# RuPaul's DRAG RACE
# UK REVISITED

RYAN VALMONT

Copyright © 2023 Ryan Valmont

All rights reserved.

# CONTENTS

INTRODUCTION ........................................................................... 1
BACKGROUND ............................................................................. 3
BROADCASTERS .......................................................................... 7
  World of Wonder ..................................................................... 7
  BBC Three ................................................................................. 8
JUDGING PANEL ........................................................................ 10
  RuPaul ..................................................................................... 11
  Michelle Visage ...................................................................... 17
  Graham Norton ...................................................................... 24
  Alan Carr ................................................................................. 28
RUPAUL'S DRAG RACE UK SERIES 1 ........................................ 32
RUPAUL'S DRAG RACE UK SERIES 2 ........................................ 67
RUPAUL'S DRAG RACE UK SERIES 3 ...................................... 107
RUPAUL'S DRAG RACE UK SERIES 4 ...................................... 147
RUPAUL'S DRAG RACE: UK VS THE WORLD – SEASON ONE .... 184
QUIZ ........................................................................................ 188
DISCLAIMER ............................................................................ 190
QUIZ ANSWERS ....................................................................... 191

# INTRODUCTION

Step into the dazzling world of high heels, glittering gowns, and fierce competition as we embark on a thrilling journey through the vibrant phenomenon that is " RuPaul's Drag Race UK." A phenomenon that transcends mere reality television and becomes a testament to the power of self-expression, individuality, and unapologetic glamour.

In a partnership between broadcasting titans "World of Wonder" and the charismatic "BBC Three," Drag Race UK emerged as a spectacular spectacle like no other. A fusion of style, wit, and sheer audacity, this show has captured the hearts of millions across the nation and beyond, redefining the boundaries of what it means to truly be oneself.

Guiding us through this electrifying adventure are the voices that matter most – the resplendent judging panel that lends its keen eye and sharp tongue to the contestants' transformative journeys. The indomitable RuPaul, a living legend whose charisma, uniqueness, nerve, and talent have become the cornerstones of this cultural revolution, is joined by the incisive Michelle Visage, the irreverently hilarious Graham Norton, and the fabulous Alan Carr. Together, they form an ensemble that brings laughter, insight, and a whole lot of sass to the runway.

As we traverse the seasons, from the inaugural Season 1, we witness the evolution of drag excellence. From lip-sync battles that send shivers down your spine to the heart-rending stories of triumph over adversity, each season encapsulates a kaleidoscope of emotions, performances, and jaw-dropping transformations that will leave you breathless.

But the excitement doesn't stop there. Brace yourself for the ultimate showdown as "RuPaul's Drag Race: UK vs the World" takes centre stage. International flair collides in a dazzling display of talent, wit, and charisma as drag artists from across the globe compete for supremacy. Who will sashay away, and who will snatch the crown in this cross-continental clash?

And dear reader, the curtain hasn't fallen yet. Prepare to test your knowledge and become the ultimate Drag Race aficionado with our spellbinding quiz. From runway revelations to iconic catchphrases, this quiz will separate the superfans from the casual viewers – do you have what it takes to claim the title?

So, fasten your seatbelts, unleash your inner diva, and get ready to experience the glitz, the glamour, and the jaw-dropping fierceness of " RuPaul's Drag Race UK." Your front-row seat to the world of sequins and stilettos awaits – let the fierce competition begin!

# BACKGROUND

RuPaul's Drag Race originated in the United States as a replacement for Rick & Steve: The Happiest Gay Couple in All the World (2007-2009). It has since been adapted in various countries, aiming to find the next "Drag Superstar" who embodies charisma, uniqueness, nerve, and talent. The show seeks entertainers who can stand out from the rest and celebrates the feeling of being an outsider.

In 2014, there were talks of Jonathan Ross hosting a UK version of Drag Race, with UK drag queen Jodie Harsh and Katie Price as judges. However, production was halted due to Ross's family issues. In 2015, Ross and Price assisted RuPaul in a one-off search for the "UK Drag Race Ambassador," won by The Vivienne. Production of the show faced obstacles as TV producers doubted its potential viewership.

During Michelle Visage's time on Celebrity Big Brother, she expressed the abundance of talent in the UK and her determination to bring Drag Race to the country. Channel 5 showed interest in broadcasting the show in 2018, and the American producers hinted at a British version. A meeting between Fenton Bailey, Randy Barbato, RuPaul, and the BBC confirmed the development of a UK version. Visage played a crucial role in making it happen, driven by the love and passion for Drag Race in the UK's LGBTQIA+ community. The show found its home at the BBC and became a huge hit, demonstrating its universal appeal.

The show was commissioned by Fiona Campbell and Kate Phillips from BBC Three and BBC Entertainment, with executive producers including RuPaul Charles, Fenton Bailey, Randy Barbato, Tom Campbell, Sally Miles, and Bruce McCoy. The BBC commissioning editor is Ruby Kuraishe. Bailey considers the UK version of Drag Race a turning point, highlighting its universal appeal.

RuPaul's Drag Race UK premiered on the 3$^{rd}$ of October 2019 and is a collaboration between the BBC, World of Wonder, and Gallowgate Productions. The show, hosted by RuPaul, follows the search for "the United Kingdom's next drag superstar." RuPaul serves as the host, mentor, and head judge alongside Michelle Visage, Alan Carr, and Graham Norton.

The series was renewed for multiple seasons, with the second season facing a production suspension due to the COVID-19 pandemic. It resumed later in 2020 and premiered in January 2021. The show received critical acclaim in the UK and garnered a large streaming audience. Its success significantly influenced the BBC's decision to bring back BBC Three. The spin-off show, RuPaul's Drag Race: UK vs the World, relaunched BBC Three with high viewership.

RuPaul's Drag Race UK has had a cultural impact, allowing contestants to enter the music and modelling industries. Groups like Frock Destroyers and United Kingdolls formed on the show, charted on the Official UK Charts. Bimini Bon-Boulash became the first drag queen from any Drag Race franchise to sign a major mainstream record deal. The show also produced the spin-off series God Shave the Queens, which follows the Drag Race contestants on tour.

The success of RuPaul's Drag Race UK led to the BBC acquiring broadcasting rights for Canada's Drag Race and RuPaul's Drag Race Down Under.

RuPaul takes on multiple roles in the show, serving as the host, coach, and judge. As the host, he introduces celebrity guests, announces the weekly challenges, and reveals the eliminated contestant. In his coaching role, RuPaul provides guidance and support to the contestants throughout the challenges. As a judge, he offers critiques on the queens' overall performance in each challenge.

The show follows a progressive elimination format, starting with a field of ten contestants (in the first series) and narrowing it down through each episode. The final three queens compete in the ultimate challenge, with the final two engaging in a lip-sync battle for the crown. Each episode follows a structured format, including a mini-challenge, a main challenge, a runway walk featuring themed fashion, the judging panel's evaluation, a lip-sync battle, and the elimination of a contestant.

## MINI CHALLENGES

Mini-challenges in RuPaul's Drag Race UK involve contestants performing various tasks with specific requirements and time constraints. Some mini-challenges are repeated throughout the series or are inspired by the original American version. For example, the first mini-challenge often involves a photo shoot with a twist, such as being drenched with water or posing on a trampoline. In the UK version, the queens had to manipulate their own heads using Green Screen technology.

Another recurring mini-challenge is the "reading" challenge, where contestants make comedic and often cheeky observations about their peers, drawing inspiration from the drag culture showcased in the documentary film Paris Is Burning. The winner of a mini-challenge may receive an advantage in the main challenge. While most episodes include a mini-challenge, there are select episodes where it does not occur.

## MAXI CHALLENGES AND RUNWAYS

The maxi challenges in RuPaul's Drag Race UK vary in their requirements and can be either individual or group challenges. The winner of the maxi challenge receives a special prize, such as a humorous "RuPeter Badge" inspired by the CBBC's Blue Peter badge, awarded for exceptional performance. In the final maxi challenge, the queens participate in an all-singing and all-dancing routine to one of RuPaul's songs.

Each maxi challenge presents a new theme and objective. Contestants are often tasked with designing and creating custom outfits, sometimes using unconventional materials. Other challenges focus on the contestants' camera presence, musical performances, or comedic skills. Certain challenges have become traditions throughout the series, such as the iconic "Snatch Game," where contestants impersonate celebrities in a recreation of the game show Match Game. Other recurring challenges include balls, where contestants showcase different themed outfits, and makeovers, where they transform individuals into drag personas.

During the runway portion of the show, contestants present their outfits to the judges. If the maxi challenge involves creating an outfit, it is showcased on the runway. Otherwise, contestants are assigned a theme and must put together a look that aligns with the theme. The runway looks and presentation are judged alongside the maxi challenge performance, determining the overall success of each contestant.

# BROADCASTERS

## WORLD OF WONDER

World of Wonder Productions, founded in 1991 by filmmakers Randy Barbato and Fenton Bailey, is an American production company based in Los Angeles, California. Specialising in documentary television and film productions, World of Wonder has gained recognition for its focus on LGBTQ topics. The company has produced programming for various networks, including HBO, Bravo, HGTV, Showtime, BBC, Netflix, MTV, and VH1. Some of their notable credits include the Million Dollar Listing docuseries, RuPaul's Drag Race, and documentary films like Mapplethorpe: Look at the Pictures and The Eyes of Tammy Faye.

World of Wonder has significantly contributed to LGBTQ programming and was awarded an Outfest Annual Achievement Award in 2011. One of their most well-known productions is RuPaul's Drag Race, which they have produced alongside managing the career of RuPaul for many years. They have also produced live shows, podcasts, television specials, and conventions associated with the Drag Race franchise.

The company was co-founded by Fenton Bailey and Randy Barbato, who met in NYU's graduate film program in the mid-1980s. They initially formed a disco-pop rock duo called the Fabulous Pop Tarts and later ventured into television production, documentary filmmaking, and artist management. World of Wonder operates from a historic building on Hollywood Boulevard and has garnered multiple Emmy nominations and wins for their television and documentary programming.

In addition to their television productions, World of Wonder has produced feature-length documentaries on various subjects, including Inside Deep Throat, Wishful Drinking, and Becoming Chaz. They have also ventured into new media types, such as conventions (RuPaul's DragCon) and the subscription streaming service WOW Presents Plus. The company's YouTube channel, WOWPresents, has a substantial following and features a wide range of content.

Overall, World of Wonder Productions has left a significant impact on the entertainment industry, particularly in the realm of LGBTQ programming and documentary filmmaking.

## BBC THREE

BBC Three is specifically geared towards a youth-oriented audience, aiming to provide innovative programming for viewers aged 16 to 34. Unlike its commercial counterparts, the channel predominantly showcases content originating from the United Kingdom. However, it does feature a few exceptions, such as shows like Family Guy and American Dad, which are from the United States. Additionally, BBC Three and its sister channel, BBC Four, occasionally broadcast BBC Sports programming as overflow content for the BBC's other channels.

The channel faced budget cuts at the BBC, leading to its initial closure on the 16$^{th}$ of February 2016. It then transformed into an online-only service available through the BBC iPlayer. However, plans were later announced to reintroduce BBC Three as a late-night strand on BBC One from Monday to Wednesday nights, beginning on the 4$^{th}$ of March 2019. In March 2021, the BBC confirmed its intention to relaunch BBC Three as a linear television channel in 2022, and the proposal was approved in November of the same year.

On the 1st of February 2022, BBC Three officially returned to linear television, sharing its broadcasting hours with CBBC. The channel now operates from 7:00 p.m. to 4:00 a.m., featuring pre-watershed programming targeting teenagers as part of its schedule. Its relaunch included a line-up of shows such as RuPaul's Drag Race: UK vs the World, Lazy Susan, and Cherry Valentine: Gypsy Queen and Proud.

# JUDGING PANEL

A panel of judges provides feedback on the contestants' performances in the challenges and their runway looks. The judges share their opinions while the contestants are onstage and also discuss them offstage.

In the UK version, RuPaul serves as both the host and main judge, just like in the original American version. Michelle Visage consistently joins RuPaul on the judging panel in every episode. Graham Norton and Alan Carr take turns as rotating supporting judges, typically appearing in one episode each. In the seventh episode of the fourth series, RuPaul was absent from the panel, and Visage acted as the stand-in host and main judge.

Series 1 featured guest judges such as Maisie Williams, Geri Halliwell, Jade Thirlwall, Andrew Garfield, Michaela Coel, Cheryl, and Twiggy. MNEK and AJ & Curtis Pritchard served as guest vocalists and choreographers during themed tasks. Dawn French revealed herself as the first guest judge for the second series. French shared that she was originally approached to be a full-time judge for the first series but couldn't commit due to living outside of London. However, she made appearances as a guest judge. French also mentioned that for the second series, each judge would sit on their own panel due to COVID-19 restrictions, with a sort of Perspex barrier between them.

# RUPAUL

RuPaul Andre Charles (born 17th of November 1960) is a multi-talented American personality renowned for his drag queen persona. He excels as a television personality, actor, musician, model, and producer. RuPaul gained widespread fame as the creator, host, and judge of the popular reality competition series RuPaul's Drag Race. Throughout his career, he has been honoured with numerous awards, including 12 Primetime Emmy Awards, three GLAAD Media Awards, a Critics' Choice Television Award, two Billboard Music Awards, and a Tony Award. His remarkable contributions to the drag community have earned him the title "Queen of Drag."

| Year | Studio Albums |
|---|---|
| 1993 | Supermodel of the World |
| 1996 | Foxy Lady |
| 1997 | Ho Ho Ho |
| 2004 | Red Hot |
| 2009 | Champion |
| 2011 | Glamazon |
| 2014 | Born Naked |
| 2015 | Realness |
| 2015 | Slay Belles |
| 2016 | Butch Queen |
| 2017 | American |
| 2018 | Christmas Party |
| 2020 | You're a Winner, Baby |
| 2022 | Mamaru |
| 2023 | Black Butta |

RuPaul was born and raised in San Diego, but later pursued studies in performing arts in Atlanta. He eventually settled in New York City, where he became an influential figure in the LGBT nightclub scene. He achieved international recognition as a drag queen with the release of his debut single, "Supermodel (You Better Work)," which was featured on his first studio album, Supermodel of the World, released in 1993. Notably, RuPaul made history as the first drag queen to secure a major cosmetics campaign, serving as a spokesperson for MAC Cosmetics in 1994. Through his collaboration with MAC, he raised funds for the Mac AIDS Fund. Additionally, RuPaul hosted his own talk show, The RuPaul Show, on VH1 for over 100 episodes while co-hosting the morning radio show on WKTU alongside Michelle Visage.

In 2009, RuPaul created RuPaul's Drag Race, a ground-breaking television show that has spawned several seasons in the United States. The show's success has extended beyond national borders, with international versions like RuPaul's Drag Race UK and Canada's Drag Race. It has also inspired various spin-offs, including RuPaul's Drag U, RuPaul's Drag Race All Stars, and RuPaul's Secret Celebrity Drag Race. RuPaul has expanded his television presence as a host on other reality series such as Skin Wars, Good Work, and Gay for Play Game Show.

| Year | Film | Role |
| --- | --- | --- |
| 1987 | RuPaul Is: Starbooty! | Starbooty |
| 1994 | Crooklyn | Connie |
| 1995 | The Brady Bunch Movie | Mrs. Cummings |
| 1995 | Wigstock: The Movie | Himself |
| 1995 | Blue in the Face | Dancer |
| 1995 | To Wong Foo, Thanks for Everything! Julie Newmar | Rachel Tensions |
| 1995 | Red Ribbon Blues | Duke |
| 1995 | A Mother's Prayer | Deacon "Dede" |
| 1996 | Fled | Himself |
| 1996 | A Very Brady Sequel | Mrs. Cummings |
| 1998 | An Unexpected Life | Charles |
| 1999 | EDtv | Himself |
| 1999 | But I'm a Cheerleader | Mike |
| 2000 | The Eyes of Tammy Faye | Narrator |

| 2000 | The Truth About Jane | Jimmy |
| --- | --- | --- |
| 2000 | For the Love of May | Jimbo |
| 2001 | Who is Cletis Tout? | Ginger Markum |
| 2005 | Dangerous Liaisons | Himself |
| 2006 | Zombie Prom: The Movie | Delilah Strict |
| 2007 | Starrbooty | Starrbooty/Cupcake |
| 2008 | Another Gay Sequel: Gays Gone Wild | Tyrell Tyrelle |
| 2016 | Hurricane Bianca | Weather Man |
| 2018 | Show Dogs | Persephone (voice) |
| 2019 | Someone Great | Hype |
| 2019 | Trixie Mattel: Moving Parts | Himself |
| 2021 | The Bitch Who Stole Christmas | Hannah Contour |
| 2022 | Zombies 3 | The Mothership (voice) |
| 2022 | Hitpig | (voice) |
| 2023 | Nimona | TBA (Voice) |
| 2023 | Trolls Band Together | Miss Maxine (voice) |

Beyond television, RuPaul has made notable appearances in films like Crooklyn (1994), The Brady Bunch Movie (1995), To Wong Foo, Thanks for Everything! Julie Newmar (1995), But I'm a Cheerleader (1999), and television shows like Girlboss (2017), Broad City (2017), and Grace and Frankie (2019). He further ventured into creating and starring in his own Netflix original series, AJ and the Queen, which premiered in 2020. Additionally, RuPaul has authored three books: Lettin' It All Hang Out (1995), Workin' It! RuPaul's Guide to Life, Liberty, and the Pursuit of Style (2010), and GuRu (2018).

RuPaul's immense success in the United States has established him as the most commercially successful drag queen in the country. He has been recognised as "easily the world's most famous drag queen" by Fortune magazine. For his remarkable contributions to RuPaul's Drag Race, he has received 12 Primetime Emmy Awards, making him the most-awarded person of colour in the history of the Primetime Emmys. In 2017, he was included in Time magazine's annual Time 100 list, recognising the most influential people in the world. Alongside his work in film and television, RuPaul continues to pursue music, having released multiple studio albums. He also earned a Tony Award as a producer for the musical A Strange Loop.

| Year | TV | Role |
| --- | --- | --- |
| 1988 | The Gong Show | Himself |
| 1993 | Saturday Night Live | Himself |
| 1994 | Sister, Sister | Marje |
| 1995 | In the House | Kevin |
| 1996–98 | The RuPaul Show | Himself |
| 1996–98 | Nash Bridges | Simone Dubois |
| 1998 | Hercules | Rock Guardian |
| 1998 | Sabrina, the Teenage Witch | The Witch Judge / Hair Dresser |
| 1998 | Walker, Texas Ranger | Bob |
| 2001 | Popular | Sweet Honey Child |
| 2001 | Port Charles | Madame Alicia |
| 2001 | Weakest Link | Himself |
| 2002 | Son of the Beach | Heinous Anus |
| 2006 | Top Chef: San Francisco | Himself |
| 2008 | Project Runway | Himself |
| 2009 | Rick & Steve: The Happiest Gay Couple in All the World | Tyler |
| 2009–present | RuPaul's Drag Race | Himself |
| 2010 | Ugly Betty | Rudolph |
| 2010–12 | RuPaul's Drag U | Himself |
| 2012–present | RuPaul's Drag Race All Stars | Himself |
| 2013 | Happy Endings | Krisjahn |
| 2013 | Life With La Toya | Himself |
| 2013 | Lady Gaga and the Muppets Holiday Spectacular | Himself |
| 2014 | The Face | Himself |
| 2014 | Mystery Girls | Emillo |
| 2014 | The Comeback | Himself |
| 2014–16 | Skin Wars | Himself |
| 2015 | Harvey Beaks | Jackie Slitherstein |

| | | |
|---|---|---|
| 2015 | Good Work | Host |
| 2015 | Bubble Guppies | Drag Snail/Costume Boxing Judge |
| 2016 | The Muppets | Himself |
| 2016–17 | Gay for Play Game Show Starring RuPaul | Host |
| 2016 | The Real O'Neals | Himself |
| 2017 | 2 Broke Girls | Himself |
| 2017 | Animals. | Dr. Labcoat (out of drag) |
| 2017 | Girlboss | Lionel |
| 2017 | Then and Now with Andy Cohen | Himself |
| 2017 | BoJack Horseman | Queen Antonia |
| 2017 | Broad City | Marcel |
| 2017 | Adam Ruins Everything | Gil |
| 2018 | Drag Race Thailand | Himself |
| 2018 | The Ellen DeGeneres Show | Himself |
| 2018 | The Simpsons | Queen Chante (voice) |
| 2019 | The Bravest Knight | Stanley the Big Bad Wolf (in drag) |
| 2019 | The World's Best | Himself |
| 2019 | Grace and Frankie | Benjamin Le Day |
| 2019 | RuPaul | Himself |
| 2019–present | RuPaul's Drag Race UK | Himself |
| 2020 | AJ and the Queen | Ruby Red |
| 2020 | Saturday Night Live | Himself |
| 2020–present | RuPaul's Secret Celebrity Drag Race | Himself |
| 2020 | The Price Is Right at Night[51] | Himself |
| 2020–present | Canada's Drag Race | Himself |
| 2020 | Muppets Now | Himself |
| 2020–present | Drag Race Holland | Himself |
| 2020 | Earth to Ned | Himself |
| 2021–present | RuPaul's Drag Race Down Under | Himself |
| 2021 | Jimmy Kimmel Live! | Himself |
| 2021 | Chicago Party Aunt | Gideon (voice) |
| 2021 | Drag Race Italia | Himself |
| 2021–2022 | Amphibia | Mr. X (voice) |
| 2021–2022 | Painted with Raven | Himself |
| 2022 | RuPaul's Drag Race: UK vs the World | Himself |
| 2022 | Drag Race Philippines | Himself |

| 2022 | Ant & Dec's Saturday Night Takeaway | Himself |
|---|---|---|
| 2022 | The Late Late Show with James Corden | Himself |
| 2022 | Celebrity Lingo | Himself |
| 2022 | The Tiny Chef Show | Announcer (voice) |
| 2022 | Canada's Drag Race: Canada vs. the World | Himself |

# MICHELLE VISAGE

Michelle Lynn Shupack (born 20th September 1968) known professionally as Michelle Visage, is a multifaceted American entertainer. Born and raised in New Jersey, Visage grew up with the knowledge that she was adopted from an early age. Her adoptive parents, who were Jewish, raised her in the Jewish faith. Her biological father was also Jewish, while her biological mother had Irish and Italian Catholic heritage. Despite growing up in a predominantly non-Jewish community, her parents made sure she had the opportunity to attend Hebrew school and have a Bat Mitzvah. She completed her high school education at South Plainfield High School in South Plainfield, New Jersey, graduating in 1986. At the age of 16, Visage won a Madonna lookalike competition, and this experience motivated her to move to New York City and pursue a career in acting. She attended the American Musical and Dramatic Academy in Manhattan for two years. Throughout her upbringing, Visage admired artists such as Madonna, Belinda Carlisle, Pat Benatar, Stevie Nicks, Cyndi Lauper, and Dale Bozzio.

In New York City, Visage immersed herself in the vibrant club scene, becoming highly involved in the drag ball scene. Visage collaborated with Cesar Valentino, and together, they showcased voguing on the television show The Latin Connection in 1988, marking the first national TV appearance of voguing.

| Year | Song | Group |
|---|---|---|
| 1989 | Nothing Matters Without Love (Album) | Seduction |
| 1992 | It's Gonna Be a Lovely Day | The S.O.U.L. S.Y.S.T.E.M. |
| 2021 | Heartbreak in This City | Steps |

During her time in the New York ball scene, Visage adopted the surname "Visage" after being called "cara" (Spanish for "face") by the people she associated with. However, due to mispronunciations, she decided to change it to "visage" (French for "face")—a language she had studied during middle and high school. From that point onward, she has continued to use the name Visage. It was in the late 1980s when Visage first encountered her future friend and co-star RuPaul, attending club nights and parties hosted by Susanne Bartsch. In 1989, Visage performed at "The Love Ball," a charity event organised by Bartsch in support of the Design Industries Foundation for AIDS. It is said that Madonna witnessed voguing for the first time at The Love Ball, inspiring her iconic song "Vogue". During the day, Visage worked as a receptionist at Casablanca and Fundamental Things, shops located in the New York garment district.

Visage auditioned and secured a spot in Seduction, an R&B and dance vocal trio assembled by Robert Clivilles and David Cole, who signed with A&M Records in 1990. Seduction had several hits, including their most popular song, "Two to Make It Right". After the group disbanded, Visage collaborated with the freestyle dance act TKA as a guest vocalist on the track "Crash (Have Some Fun)". Additionally, Visage provided lead vocals and served as the recording artist for another dance act formed by Clivilles and Cole called The S.O.U.L. S.Y.S.T.E.M. Their rendition of the Bill Withers song "Lovely Day" titled "It's Gonna Be a Lovely Day" was featured on The Bodyguard soundtrack. The song reached number one on the dance charts and peaked at number 34 on the Billboard Hot 100 in January 1993.

Visage has also appeared in various music albums by RuPaul and featured in music videos such as "New York City Beat" and "From Your Heart," which premiered on RuPaul's Green Screen Christmas Special in 2015 and were subsequently shared on World of Wonder's YouTube channel. She has made guest appearances in music videos for RuPaul's songs "Glamazon," "Responsitrannity," "The Beginning," and "Nothing for Christmas".

In February 2021, it was confirmed that Visage collaborated with Steps on a revised version of "Heartbreak In This City".

In the realm of radio, Visage co-hosted the morning show on WKTU in New York City from 1996 to 2002, where she began working professionally with RuPaul. When RuPaul left the radio, Visage continued hosting various morning shows, including Hot 92 Jamz (KHHT) in Los Angeles from 2002 to 2005. She returned to New York City in 2005 and served as co-host of The Morning Mix on WNEW-FM until December 2006. She also hosted The Beat 66 on Sirius Satellite Radio from 2003 to 2006. In March 2007, she became a co-host of the morning show on SUNNY 104.3 in West Palm Beach, Florida. In January 2011, she joined 93.9 MIA in Miami as the host of the new MIA Morning Show. After leaving Miami and MIA in December 2011, she moved back to Los Angeles.

From April 2014, Visage co-hosted the weekly podcast "RuPaul: What's the Tee?" with RuPaul. In this podcast, they interview celebrities and discuss a wide range of topics, including their personal lives and RuPaul's Drag Race. The podcast received a Webby Award in 2018. Visage also presented "Michelle Visage's Fabulous Divas" on BBC Radio 2, with episodes airing in December 2019 and August 2020. In October and November 2020, she filled in for Rylan Clark on his BBC Radio 2 show, and in February 2022, she covered for Dermot O'Leary on his Saturday weekend breakfast show. As of July 2022, she began hosting her own show every Friday night from 7 to 9 pm on BBC Radio 2.

Throughout her career, Visage has collaborated with RuPaul on several television shows. In 1996, she became the co-host of RuPaul's VH1 talk show, The RuPaul Show. She also co-hosted WKTU's morning show with RuPaul from 1996 to 2002. When RuPaul began casting judges for the first season of RuPaul's Drag Race, he invited Visage to join the show as a permanent member.

Despite her boss initially rejecting the offer due to the show's association with the LGBTQ+ community, Visage sought permission from CBS officials, ultimately allowing her to become a judge on the show. In January 2011, Visage made her debut as a permanent judge alongside Santino Rice and Billy B on the third season of RuPaul's Drag Race, replacing Merle Ginsberg. She has also appeared on all seasons of the spin-off series RuPaul's Drag Race All Stars.

| Year | Title | Genre | Role |
|---|---|---|---|
| 1989 | Dance Party USA | Television | Herself |
| 1990 | Club MTV | Television | Herself |
| 1996–1998 | The RuPaul Show | Television | Herself |
| 2002 | Maybe It's Me | Movie | Tania |
| 2011–present | RuPaul's Drag Race | Television | Herself |
| 2011–present | RuPaul's Drag Race: Untucked | Television | Herself |
| 2012–present | RuPaul's Drag Race: All Stars | Television | Herself |
| 2013 | That Sex Show | Television | Herself |
| 2013–2015 | The Most Popular Girls in School | Web Series | Mrs. Zales |
| 2015 | Celebrity Big Brother 15 | Television | Herself |
| 2017 | Eurovision Song Contest | Television | Commentator |
| 2018–2019 | Ireland's Got Talent | Television | Herself |
| 2018 | The X Factor | Television | Herself |
| 2018–2019 | Everybody's Talking About Jamie | Theatre | Miss Hedge |
| 2019 | The Only Way Is Essex | Television | Herself |
| 2019 | RuPaul | Television | Herself |
| 2019 | Guest Grumps | Web series | Herself |
| 2019 | Strictly Come Dancing | Television | Herself |
| 2019–present | RuPaul's Drag Race UK | Television | Herself |
| 2020 | How's Your Head, Hun? | Television | Herself |
| 2020 | Glow Up: Britain's Next Make-Up Star | Television | Herself |
| 2020 | Canada's Drag Race | Television | Herself |
| 2021 | Ant & Dec's Saturday Night Takeaway | Television | Herself |
| 2021 | RuPaul's Drag Race Down Under | Television | Herself |
| 2021 | Dragging the Classics: The Brady Bunch | Television | Helen |
| 2021 | Celebrity Gogglebox for Su2c | Television | Herself |

| 2021 | The Wendy Williams Show | Television | Herself |
| 2021 | Queen of the Universe | Television | Herself |
| 2021 | The Bitch Who Stole Christmas | Movie | Narrator |
| 2022 | RuPaul's Drag Race: UK vs the World | Television | Herself |

In 2019, Visage received her first Primetime Emmy Award for Outstanding Competition Program as a producer of Drag Race, starting from the show's eleventh season. That same year, she became a judge on RuPaul's Drag Race UK, which airs on BBC Three. In 2021, Visage served as a judge on RuPaul's Drag Race Down Under.

Visage participated as a contestant on the fifteenth series of the British reality show Celebrity Big Brother, which aired on Channel 5. She entered the house on the 7th of January 2015 and finished in fifth place on 6th of February 2015. After her time in the house, she made appearances on some episodes of Celebrity Big Brother's Bit on the Side, a companion show that airs immediately after Celebrity Big Brother.

| Participant | Age (at time of filming) | Profession | Result |
| --- | --- | --- | --- |
| Katie Price | 36 | TV personality & glamour model | 1st – Winner |
| Katie Hopkins | 39 | TV personality and columnist | 2nd – Runner-up |
| Calum Best | 33 | Model and TV personality | 3rd – Third place |
| Keith Chegwin | 57 | Actor and presenter | 4th – Evicted |
| **Michelle Visage** | **46** | **Singer and presenter** | **5th – Evicted** |
| Perez Hilton | 36 | Blogger and TV personality | 6th – Evicted |
| Kavana | 37 | Singer | 7th – Evicted |
| Cami-Li | 26 | Model | 8th – Evicted |
| Nadia Sawalha | 50 | Actress and presenter | 9th – Evicted |
| Patsy Kensit | 46 | Actress | 10th – Evicted |
| Alicia Douvall | 35 | Media personality | 11th – Evicted |
| Alexander O'Neal | 61 | Singer | 12th – Walked |
| Chloe Goodman | 21 | Reality TV star | 13th – Evicted |
| Ken Morley | 72 | Actor | 14th – Ejected |
| Jeremy Jackson | 34 | Actor | 15th – Ejected |

Visage has made various other TV appearances, including hosting VH1's red-carpet coverage of the 1998 Grammy Awards and co-hosting Grease's 25th-anniversary re-release party in 2002. In May 2017, she and Ross Mathews provided commentary for Logo TV's coverage of the live grand final of the Eurovision Song Contest. More recently, she served as a judge on the first two seasons of Ireland's Got Talent, the first of which premiered on TV3 in February 2018. In 2020, Visage joined fellow Ireland's Got Talent judge Louis Walsh on the judging panel of the teen recycled-fashion competition Junk Kouture. She appeared on the televised grand final in February 2021, after the original live grand final plans were disrupted by COVID-19.

On the 5th of August 2019, it was announced that Visage would be participating in the seventeenth series of the UK's Strictly Come Dancing on BBC. It was later confirmed that her dance partner would be Giovanni Pernice. Visage participated for nine weeks, ultimately being eliminated with 32 points obtained from her version of Vogue.

| Week | Dance/Song | Judge's score | | | | Total | Result |
|---|---|---|---|---|---|---|---|
| | | Horwood | Mabuse | Ballas | Tonioli | | |
| 1 | Cha-Cha-Cha / "So Emotional" | 8 | 8 | 7 | 7 | 30 | No Elimination |
| 2 | Viennese Waltz / "That's Amore" | 8 | 8 | 8 | 8 | 32 | Safe |
| 3 | Quickstep / "Cabaret" | 8 | 9 | 9 | 9 | 35 | Safe |
| 4 | Salsa / "Quimbara" | 7 | 8 | 8 | 8 | 31 | Safe |
| 5 | Rumba / "Too Good at Goodbyes" | 7 | 7 | 7 | 8 | 29 | Safe |
| 6 | Foxtrot / "*The Addams Family* Theme" | 9 | 10 | 10 | 10 | 39 | Safe |
| 7 | Paso Doble / "Another One Bites The Dust" | 8 | 9 | 9 | 8 | 34 | Safe |
| 8 | American Smooth / "I Just Want to Make Love to You" | 9 | 9 | 9 | 9 | 36 | Bottom two |
| 9 | Street / "Vogue" | 8 | 8 | 8 | 8 | *32* | Eliminated |

From October 2018 to January 2019, Visage made her West End debut as "Miss Hedge" in Everybody's Talking About Jamie.

# GRAHAM NORTON

Graham William Walker (born 4th April 1963) better known by his stage name Graham Norton, is a well-known Irish actor, author, comedian, commentator, and presenter who is best known for his work in the UK. He is a five-time BAFTA TV award winner for his comedy chat show, "The Graham Norton Show", which has been airing since 2007 and has received an overall eight awards. He took over the prestigious late-Friday-evening slot on BBC One from Jonathan Ross in 2010. From 2010 to 2020, Norton hosted a Saturday morning slot on BBC Radio 2, and in 2021, he started presenting on Saturdays and Sundays on Virgin Radio UK.

Prior to his career as a presenter, Norton appeared in three episodes of the award-winning show "Father Ted" as Father Noel Furlong. In 2012, he sold his production company, So Television to ITV for around £17 million.

| Year | Film | Role |
|---|---|---|
| 1999 | Stargay | Graham Solex |
| 2006 | Another Gay Movie | Mr. Puckov |
| 2007 | I Could Never Be Your Woman | Taylor |
| 2016 | Absolutely Fabulous: The Movie | Himself |
| 2020 | Eurovision Song Contest: The Story of Fire Saga | Himself |
| 2020 | Soul | Moonwind (voice) |
| 2020 | The Stand In | Himself |

Graham Norton began his career on the BBC in 2001 by hosting Comic Relief. In 2005, he hosted the Saturday evening reality TV series "Strictly Dance Fever" and the comedy chat show "Graham Norton's Bigger Picture" on BBC One. He also read stories on the BBC children's channel CBeebies. In 2006, he presented the series "How Do You Solve a Problem like Maria?" and subsequently hosted the follow-up series "Any Dream Will Do," "I'd Do Anything," and "Over the Rainbow." Norton also hosted various other shows for the BBC, including "When Will I Be Famous?", "The One and Only", and "Totally Saturday."

He also regularly hosted the British Academy Television Awards since 2007. In May 2010, he stood in for Chris Evans' breakfast show on BBC Radio 2 and later replaced Jonathan Ross's Saturday morning slot on the same station. In December 2011, the panel show "Would You Rather...? with Graham Norton" premiered on BBC America. In February 2019, it was announced that Norton would be a judge on "RuPaul's Drag Race UK" alongside Alan Carr, Michelle Visage, and RuPaul.

In 2007, Graham Norton co-hosted the first annual Eurovision Dance Contest with Claudia Winkleman in London. The format was based on the BBC's "Strictly Come Dancing" and the EBU's Eurovision Song Contest. They also hosted the 2008 contest in Glasgow, Scotland. In 2008, Norton was announced as the replacement for Terry Wogan as the presenter of the UK national selection for the Eurovision Song Contest, "Your Country Needs You." He also took over from Wogan as the British commentator for the main Eurovision Song Contest in 2009.

Norton's debut as a commentator received positive reviews from the British press for his jokes and commentary on the performances. In 2015, Norton and Petra Mede hosted the Eurovision Song Contest's Greatest Hits concert show in London to commemorate the contest's 60th anniversary. In 2020, Norton portrayed a fictionalised version of himself as the British Eurovision commentator in the Netflix film "Eurovision Song Contest: The Story of Fire Saga."

| Year | TV | Role |
|---|---|---|
| 1996 | Carnal Knowledge | Co-host |
| 1996–1998 | Father Ted | Father Noel Furlong |
| 1997 | Bring Me the Head of Light Entertainment | Himself |
| 1998–2002 | So Graham Norton | Host |
| 2001 | Rex the Runt: A Crap Day Out | The Plants voice |
| 2001 | Rex the Runt: Patio | Osvalde Halitosis voice |
| 2001 | The Kumars at No. 42 | Himself |
| 2002 | Absolutely Fabulous | Himself |
| 2002–2003 | V Graham Norton | Host |
| 2003–2004 | Tough Crowd with Colin Quinn | Himself |
| 2004–2005 | The Graham Norton Effect | Host |
| 2005 | Generation Fame | Himself |
| 2005–2006 | Graham Norton's Bigger Picture | Himself |
| 2005–2006 | Strictly Dance Fever | Himself |
| 2006 | The Last Ever, Ever Footballers' Wives | Brendan Spunk |
| 2006 | How Do You Solve a Problem Like Maria? | Host/Presenter |
| 2007 | When Will I Be Famous? | Himself |
| 2007 | Who Do You Think You Are? | Himself |
| 2007 | Saving Planet Earth | Himself |
| 2007 | Kathy Griffin: My Life on the D-List | Himself |
| 2007 | Robbie the Reindeer | Computer voice |
| 2007 | In Close Encounters of the Herd Kind | Computer voice |
| 2007 | Live Earth | Himself |
| 2007 | Eurovision Dance Contest 2007 | Host |
| 2007–2011 | The British Academy Television Awards | Host |
| 2013–2016 | The British Academy Television Awards | Host |
| 2019 | The British Academy Television Awards | Host |
| 2007– | The Graham Norton Show | Host |
| 2007 | Any Dream Will Do | Presenter |
| 2008 | I'd Do Anything | Presenter |
| 2008 | The One and Only | Himself |
| 2008 | Eurovision Dance Contest 2008 | Host |
| 2009 | Totally Saturday | Himself |
| 2009–2010 | Eurovision: Your Country Needs You | Host |
| 2009– | Eurovision Song Contest | UK commentator/Co-presenter |

| | | |
|---|---|---|
| 2010 | Over the Rainbow | Host |
| 2011–2012 | Would You Rather...? with Graham Norton | Presenter |
| 2015 | Eurovision Song Contest's Greatest Hits | Co-presenter |
| 2015 | Adele at the BBC | Presenter |
| 2016 | RuPaul's Drag Race All Stars 2 | Himself/Guest judge |
| 2016–2019 | Children in Need | Host |
| 2017 | Let It Shine | Co-presenter |
| 2018 | The Biggest Weekend | Himself |
| 2019– | RuPaul's Drag Race UK | Himself/Judge |
| 2020 | British Academy Film Awards | Host |
| 2020 | Eurovision: Come Together | Host |
| 2020 | Eurovision: Europe Shine a Light | UK commentator |
| 2021 | Queen of the Universe | Host |
| 2021 | Celebrity Gogglebox | Himself |
| 2022– | RuPaul's Drag Race: UK vs the World | Himself/Judge |

# ALAN CARR

Alan Graham Carr is an English comedian, broadcaster, and writer who rose to prominence in 2001 when he won the City Life Best Newcomer of the Year and the BBC New Comedy Awards. He initially gained popularity on the Manchester comedy circuit and later co-hosted The Friday Night Project with Justin Lee Collins from 2006 to 2009. This led to the creation of his short-lived entertainment show, Alan Carr's Celebrity Ding Dong, in 2008. Carr's most well-known work is hosting the comedy chat show Alan Carr: Chatty Man, which aired on Channel 4 from 2009 to 2016. He has also appeared as a team captain on 8 Out of 10 Cats Does Countdown since 2017 and served as a judge on RuPaul's Drag Race UK. In 2021, Carr took over as the host of BBC's Interior Design Masters, succeeding Fearne Cotton.

| Year | Stand Up Tour |
| --- | --- |
| 2006–07 | Tooth Fairy Live |
| 2010–11 | Spexy Beast |
| 2015 | Yap, Yap, Yap! Live |
| 2021-2022 | Regional Trinket |
| 2022 | Not Again, Alan! |

Carr has had a diverse career beyond television. He hosted the radio show Going Out with Alan Carr on BBC Radio 2 from 2009 to 2012. Additionally, he has released an autobiography titled Look Who It Is! (2008) and embarked on three arena stand-up comedy tours: Tooth Fairy Live (2007), Spexy Beast Live (2011), and Yap, Yap, Yap! (2015). Carr has received several accolades for his contributions to comedy, including three British Comedy Awards, two National Television Awards, and a BAFTA TV Award.

Born on 14th of June 1976, in Weymouth, Dorset, Alan Carr is the eldest son of Christine and Graham Carr. He spent most of his childhood in Northampton, where his father worked as a football manager and chief scout. Carr has a younger brother named Gary. He attended Weston Favell Upper School in Northampton and graduated from Middlesex University with a 2:1 BA (Hons) degree in Drama and Theatre Studies.

| Year | Film | Role |
| --- | --- | --- |
| 2007 | Tooth Fairy Live | Himself |
| 2009 | Nativity! | Critic |
| 2011 | Spexy Beast Live | Himself |
| 2015 | The SpongeBob Movie: Sponge Out of Water | Seagull (voice) |
| 2015 | Yap, Yap, Yap! Live | Himself |

In his early twenties, Carr moved to Manchester with aspirations of becoming a comedian. He resided in Chorlton-cum-Hardy and later Stretford, both of which influenced his comedic work. Carr initially worked in a call centre while performing on the comedy circuit part-time. Eventually, he transitioned to a full-time career in comedy.

As a stand-up comedian, Carr regularly performs on tours and television shows. He became a fixture on the Manchester comedy circuit, where he collaborated with comedians such as Jason Manford, Justin Moorhouse, and John Bishop. Carr won the City Life Best Newcomer of the Year and the BBC New Comedy Awards in 2001. He has participated in three Edinburgh shows and embarked on a nationwide tour in 2007, which resulted in the release of a DVD titled Tooth Fairy Live. Carr has also performed at renowned venues like the Apollo Theatre in London and festivals such as Reading and Leeds Festivals, Latitude Festival, and Kilkenny Comedy Festival. His international appearances include performances at the Just for Laughs festival in Montreal.

| Year | TV | Role |
|---|---|---|
| 2005–2006 | 8 Out of 10 Cats | Himself |
| 2006 | The Law of the Playground | Himself |
| 2006–2009 | Friday/Sunday Night Project | Presenter |
| 2007–2008 | Alan Carr's Celebrity Ding Dong | Presenter |
| 2007, 2018 | Live at the Apollo | Presenter |
| 2008 | The Comedy Map of Britain | Himself |
| 2009–2016, 2017 | Alan Carr: Chatty Man | Presenter |
| 2009–2020 | The One Show | Guest Presenter |
| 2010–2016 | Channel 4's Comedy Gala | Presenter |
| 2010 | The New Paul O'Grady Show | Guest Presenter |
| 2011 | Who Do You Think You Are? | Himself |
| 2011 | My Favourite Joke | Himself |
| 2011–2017 | Alan Carr's Specstacular | Presenter |
| 2012 | Playing It Straight UK | Narrator |
| 2012 | Comedy World Cup | Contestant |
| 2012–present | Stand Up to Cancer | Co-Presenter |
| 2014 | Stars at Your Service | Co-Presenter |
| 2014 | The Singer Takes It All | Presenter |
| 2014 | Celebrity Deal or No Deal | Contestant |
| 2016 | Alan Carr's 12 Stars of Christmas | Presenter |
| 2016 | Alan Carr's Happy Hour | Presenter |
| 2016 | National Treasure | Himself |
| 2016, 2018 | Peter Kay's Comedy Shuffle | Himself |
| 2017–present | 8 Out of 10 Cats Does Countdown | Team Captain |
| 2017 | The Price is Right | Presenter |
| 2018 | The Remote Controller | Presenter |
| 2018 | I Don't Like Mondays | Presenter |
| 2018 | The Great Celebrity Bake Off | Himself |
| 2018 | Hollyoaks | Himself |
| 2018 | Alan Carr's Christmas Cracker | Presenter |
| 2019–present | There's Something About Movies | Presenter |
| 2019–present | RuPaul's Drag Race UK | Judge |
| 2019 | Alan Carr's Celebrity Re-Play 2019 | Presenter |
| 2020 | Meet the Richardsons | Himself |
| 2020 | Secrets of the Driving Test | Narrator |

| 2020 | Michael McIntyre's The Wheel | Contestant |
|---|---|---|
| 2020–2022 | Alan Carr's Epic Gameshow | Presenter |
| 2021–present | Interior Design Masters with Alan Carr | Presenter |
| 2021 | DNA Journey | Himself |
| 2021 | The Masked Singer UK | Guest Panellist |
| 2021 | Royal Variety Performance | Host |
| 2022 | RuPaul's Drag Race: UK vs the World | Judge |
| 2022 | Alan Carr's Adventures With Agatha Christie | Presenter |
| 2023 | Amanda And Alan's Italian Job | Co-presenter |
| 2023 | Picture Slam | Host |
| 2023 | Changing Ends | Himself |
| TBA | Mama Mia! Here We Go Again | Judge |

In terms of his personal life, Carr is openly gay but does not consider his sexuality a central aspect of his comedy. He has expressed the view that being gay does not automatically make one a role model. Carr has been comfortable with his sexuality since a young age and has been open about it. In January 2018, he married his partner of ten years, Paul Drayton, in Los Angeles, with the wedding officiated by his close friend Adele. However, Carr and Drayton announced their separation in January 2022.

# RUPAUL'S DRAG RACE UK SERIES 1

The first series of RuPaul's Drag Race UK premiered on 3$^{rd}$ of October 2019, on the BBC Three, available on BBC iPlayer, and internationally on World of Wonder's WOW Presents Plus streaming service. The season consisted of 8 episodes. The cast was announced on 21$^{st}$ of August through YouTube and Instagram.

As a publicly funded broadcaster, the BBC does not provide cash prizes or sponsorships in the programme, distinguishing it from the original American series. Instead, the winners of the weekly challenges were awarded a "Ru Peter Badge," a nod to the British children's show Blue Peter, which has a long history on the BBC. Additionally, the ultimate winner of the competition earned a fully covered trip to Hollywood, where they would have the opportunity to star in their own digital series produced by World of Wonder.

## EPISODE ONE: "THE ROYAL QUEENS"

Ten fresh queens make their entrance into the workroom. To kick things off, they are tasked with an "off with your heads" photoshoot for the mini challenge. Scaredy Kat impresses the judges and snatches the win.

For the maxi challenge, the queens are required to showcase two distinct looks on the runway. The first look should represent their status as the queen of their hometown, while the second look should be inspired by none other than Queen Elizabeth II herself.

During the runway presentations, Baga Chipz, Sum Ting Wong, and The Vivienne received commendations from the judges, ultimately leading to The Vivienne claiming victory for the challenge. On the other hand, Cheryl Hole, Gothy Kendoll, and Vinegar Strokes receive criticism, although Cheryl manages to secure her safety. This leaves Gothy Kendoll and Vinegar Strokes in the bottom two, lip-syncing for their lives to the beats of "New Rules" by Dua Lipa. Vinegar Strokes delivers a standout performance and emerges as the victor, while Gothy Kendoll sadly sashays away from the competition.

**Departure Message:** "I'm the UK's Porkchop! Love you, friends for life! x x x Gothy"

## QUEEN PROFILE: GOTHY KENDOLL

Gothy Kendoll, whose real name is Samuel David Handley, was born on 19th of June 1997, in Leicester, Leicestershire. He is a talented drag queen, DJ, and online creator. Gothy Kendoll gained recognition through his participation in the first series of RuPaul's Drag Race UK and his appearance on the inaugural season of the MTV series Celeb Ex in the City.

Handley began his drag career in 2016 and quickly made a name for himself, performing at various events and parties as a DJ. In 2019, he was selected as one of the twelve contestants for the first season of RuPaul's Drag Race UK, showcasing his unique style and talent on the show. Unfortunately, Gothy Kendoll was the first contestant to be eliminated from the competition after losing a lip sync performance of "New Rules" by Dua Lipa to Vinegar Strokes. This made him the first ever eliminated contestant on the British version of the show.

Expanding his presence in the entertainment industry, Kendoll joined the cast of the MTV reality series Celeb Ex in the City in

2020, further showcasing his personality and versatility. In 2021, he took a step into the music industry by releasing his debut single titled "Switch." The track featured vocals from his fellow RuPaul's Drag Race UK contestant, Divina de Campo, along with Forbid.

## GUEST JUDGE PROFILE: ANDREW GARFIELD

Andrew Russell Garfield, born on 20th of August 1983, is a renowned English-American actor. Throughout his career, he has received numerous accolades, including a Tony Award, a BAFTA TV Award, and a Golden Globe Award. He has also been nominated for a Primetime Emmy Award, a Laurence Olivier Award, and two Academy Awards. In 2022, Garfield was recognized by Time magazine as one of the 100 most influential people in the world.

Originally from Los Angeles, Garfield was raised in Epsom, England. He honed his acting skills at the Royal Central School of Speech and Drama, starting his career on the UK stage and in television productions. His feature film debut came in 2007 with the ensemble drama "Lions for Lambs." Garfield's performance in the television film "Boy A" (2007) earned him the BAFTA TV Award for Best Actor. He gained international prominence in 2010 with his supporting role as Eduardo Saverin in the drama "The Social Network," which garnered him BAFTA Film Award and Golden Globe Award nominations.

Garfield became widely recognised for his portrayal of Spider-Man in the superhero films "The Amazing Spider-Man" (2012), "The Amazing Spider-Man 2" (2014), and later in "Spider-Man: No Way Home" (2021). He received Academy Award nominations for Best Actor for his roles in the war film "Hacksaw Ridge" (2016) as Desmond Doss and the musical "Tick, Tick... Boom!" (2021) as

Jonathan Larson. Garfield won a Golden Globe Award for Best Actor for his performance in the latter. In 2022, he starred as a Mormon detective in the crime drama miniseries "Under the Banner of Heaven," earning nominations for a Primetime Emmy Award and a Golden Globe Award.

On stage, Garfield garnered acclaim for his appearance in the 2012 Broadway revival of "Death of a Salesman," which led to a Tony Award nomination. He received a Laurence Olivier Award nomination for his portrayal of Prior Walter in a 2017 London production of "Angels in America." Garfield reprised the role on Broadway the following year, winning the Tony Award for Best Actor in a Play.

Born in Los Angeles, Garfield's mother, Lynn (née Hillman), hailed from Essex, England, while his father, Richard Garfield, is from California. The family relocated to the United Kingdom when he was three years old, and he grew up in Epsom, Surrey. Garfield describes himself as a "Jewish artist," with his Jewish heritage coming from his father's side. His grandparents were Jewish immigrants who settled in London from Poland, Russia, and Romania. The family surname was originally "Garfinkel."

During his youth, Garfield was involved in gymnastics and swimming. Although he initially intended to study business, his interest in acting blossomed when he took theatre studies at A-level. Garfield attended Priory Preparatory School and later City of London Freemen's School before pursuing his training at the Central School of Speech and Drama, University of London. Prior to his acting career, he worked at multiple Starbucks locations in Golders Green and Hendon.

## EPISODE TWO: "DOWNTON DRAGGY"

The episode kicks off with The Vivienne, the previous challenge winner, being tasked with ranking the queens from best to worst. In her ranking, she places herself at the top and Scaredy Kat at the bottom. As a result, they are chosen as team captains for the upcoming maxi challenge. The challenge involves the queens starring in drag adaptations of the popular series "Downton Abbey," aptly titled "Downton Draggy." Scaredy Kat selects Blu Hydrangea, Cheryl Hole, Crystal, and Divina De Campo for her team. Meanwhile, The Vivienne chooses Baga Chipz, Sum Ting Wong, and Vinegar Strokes to join her team.

On the runway, the queens showcase their Bond Girl Glamourama looks. Team The Vivienne emerges as the winning team, with Baga Chipz securing the challenge victory. Unfortunately, it's a different story for Team Scaredy Kat, who end up as the losing team. Blu Hydrangea, Cheryl Hole, and Scaredy Kat receive negative critiques from the judges, although Cheryl manages to secure her safety. This leaves Blu and Scaredy in the bottom two, lip-syncing for their lives to the iconic tune "Venus" by Bananarama. In the end, Blu Hydrangea delivers a standout performance and emerges as the winner of the lip sync, while Scaredy Kat sadly sashays away from the competition.

**Departure Message:** "Scaredy the whole way. 19 now, what's gonna happen when I'm 35. :P Thanks girls. Cya later! Meowx"

## QUEEN PROFILE: SCAREDY KAT

Scaredy Kat, born Alex Cove and also credited as Ally Cubb, is a notable British drag queen, comedian, actor, and writer. Their claim to fame came from their participation in the first season of RuPaul's Drag Race UK. Notably, at the time of filming, Scaredy Kat was the youngest drag queen to compete in the British series.

In terms of personal life, Scaredy Kat stands out as one of the few queens on Drag Race who is not exclusively identified as gay. They have expressed a more fluid approach to relationships, stating that they go out with anyone they fall in love with. Their girlfriend, known as Pussy Kat, played a significant role in encouraging Scaredy Kat to explore the world of drag.

Beyond their drag persona, Scaredy Kat is passionate about veganism and animal rights activism. They have actively collaborated with PETA UK on campaigns against fur. Additionally, Scaredy Kat has made appearances on various television shows, including Channel 4's Reasons to be Cheerful with Matt Lucas and BBC Three's Pls Like.

In 2022, Scaredy Kat ventured into the world of acting and appeared in the Netflix film "The School for Good and Evil." Directed by Paul Feig, Scaredy Kat portrayed the character Gregor in the movie.

## GUEST JUDGE PROFILE: MAISIE WILLIAMS

Margaret Constance "Maisie" Williams, born on 15th of April 1997, is a talented English actress. Her breakthrough came in 2011 when she made her acting debut as Arya Stark, a prominent character in the HBO epic medieval fantasy series Game of Thrones (2011–2019). Williams garnered significant recognition and critical acclaim for her portrayal and received two Emmy Award nominations for her outstanding work on the show.

Williams has made notable appearances on various television productions. She guest-starred as Ashildr in the BBC science fiction series Doctor Who (2015) and starred in the British docudrama television film Cyberbully (2015) and the British science-fiction teen thriller film iBoy (2017). In addition, she played the central character, Kim Noakes, in the comedy action drama series Two Weeks to Live (2020) and portrayed punk rock icon Jordan (Pamela Rooke) in Pistol (2022), a biopic about the Sex Pistols. Williams also lent her voice to the character Cammie MacCloud in the American animated web series Gen: Lock (2019–2021).

Her feature film debut came in 2014 when she played Lydia in the coming-of-age mystery drama The Falling, a performance that garnered critical acclaim and awards recognition. Williams has also appeared in films such as the romantic period-drama film Mary Shelley (2017), the animated prehistorical sports comedy film Early Man (2018), and the romantic comedy-drama film Then Came You (2018). In 2020, she starred in the superhero horror film The New Mutants and the psychological thriller The Owners. Additionally, Williams made her stage debut in 2018 in Lauren Gunderson's play I and You at the Hampstead Theatre in London, receiving positive reviews from critics.

Beyond acting, Williams is an entrepreneur. In 2019, she co-developed and launched the social media platform Daisie, which serves as a multimedia networking app designed to support artists and creators, especially those starting their careers.

Known as "Maisie" from a young age, she earned the nickname due to her resemblance to a cartoon character. Williams attended Clutton Primary School and Norton Hill School in Midsomer Norton before transferring to Bath Dance College to study Performing Arts. Her passion for becoming a professional dancer led her to train in various disciplines. She left school at the age of 14 to pursue her acting career and received home education without taking formal examinations.

# EPISODE THREE: "POSH ON A PENNY"

In this week's mini-challenge, the queens showcase their captivating dance moves around a maypole. Cheryl Hole impresses the judges and emerges as the winner of the mini-challenge.

For the maxi challenge, the queens are tasked with transforming junk items found at a car boot sale into show-stopping outfits.

On the runway, Crystal, Divina De Campo, and The Vivienne receive high praise from the judges for their creative looks. Ultimately, Divina De Campo excels and emerges as the winner of the challenge. Cheryl Hole, Sum Ting Wong, and Vinegar Strokes receive critiques on their outfits, with Cheryl being deemed safe.

In the bottom two, Sum Ting Wong and Vinegar Strokes face off in a lip-sync battle to the iconic tune "Would I Lie to You?" by Eurythmics. Sum Ting Wong delivers a captivating performance, securing her victory in the lip sync. Unfortunately, Vinegar Strokes sashays away from the competition.

**Departure Message:** "Long live the OG RPDRUK SLAAAAGS! You're all amazing - Hodge Podge FOREVER! xxx"

## QUEEN PROFILE: VINEGAR STROKES

Vinegar Strokes, born 21$^{st}$ of August 1984, is the stage name of Daniel Jacob, hailing from London.

Prior to embracing the art of drag, Jacob pursued his passion for acting by studying at the Liverpool Institute for Performing Arts. However, he struggled to secure acting roles until he adopted the persona of Vinegar Strokes, which would ultimately pave the way for his successful career.

Vinegar Strokes gained significant recognition for her appearance on the inaugural season of RuPaul's Drag Race UK. Additionally, she had the privilege of performing alongside Drag Race judge Michelle Visage and Bianca Del Rio, the winner of US Drag Race, in the West End Musical production of Everybody's Talking About Jamie.

Following her stint on Drag Race, Strokes captivated audiences with her portrayal of Lady Von Fistenberg in the "camp drag murder mystery" play Death Drop.

In addition to her stage performances, Vinegar Strokes has shared her musical singles on YouTube and even hosts an online cooking series, showcasing her diverse talents and creative pursuits.

## GUEST JUDGE PROFILE: TWIGGY

Dame Lesley Lawson DBE, born Lesley Hornby on 19th September 1949, is an English model, actress, and singer, known by her nickname Twiggy. Born in Neasden, London, Twiggy was raised by her parents Nellie Lydia and William Norman Hornby. She learned to sew from her mother and attended Brondesbury and Kilburn High School. She rose to prominence as a cultural icon and a leading teenage model during the vibrant '60s in London.

Twiggy initially gained attention for her slender figure and androgynous appearance, characterised by her big eyes, long eyelashes, and short hair. She was dubbed "The Face of 1966" by the Daily Express and voted British Woman of the Year. By 1967, she had established herself as an international model, gracing the covers of Vogue and The Tatler, and modelling in France, Japan, and the US.

After her successful modelling career, Twiggy transitioned to become an accomplished actress on screen, stage, and television. Her role in the film "The Boy Friend" (1971) earned her two Golden Globe Awards. In 1983, she made her Broadway debut in the musical "My One and Only," receiving a Tony nomination for Best Actress in a Musical. Twiggy also hosted her own series, "Twiggy's People," where she interviewed celebrities, and served as a judge on "America's Next Top Model." Her autobiography, "Twiggy in Black and White" (1998), became a best-seller. Additionally, she has been a prominent model for Marks and Spencer since 2005, and collaborated with the brand on an exclusive clothing collection.

Twiggy's career continued to thrive in the following decades. She appeared in various films and TV shows, including a memorable cover collaboration with David Bowie for his album "Pin Ups" (1973). She also participated in live performances and released successful albums such as "Twiggy" and "Please Get My Name Right."

## EPISODE FOUR: "SNATCH GAME"

In the maxi challenge, the queens take on the Snatch Game with special guest judges Lorraine Kelly and Stacey Dooley. The line-up consisted of:

- Baga Chipz as Margaret Thatcher
- Blu Hydrangea as Mary Berry
- Cheryl Hole as Gemma Collins
- Crystal as Rue McClanahan
- Divina De Campo as Julia Child
- Sum Ting Wong as Sir David Attenborough
- The Vivienne as Donald Trump

For the runway, the theme is Weird Science. Baga Chipz and The Vivienne shine with their performances, receiving positive critiques and ultimately sharing the title of challenge winners. On the other hand, Crystal, Divina De Campo, and Sum Ting Wong face negative critiques. However, Divina is declared safe from elimination.

Crystal and Sum Ting Wong find themselves in the bottom two and have to lip-sync for their lives to "Spice Up Your Life" by Spice Girls. Crystal delivers an outstanding performance and emerges victorious, winning the lip sync. As a result, Sum Ting Wong is asked to sashay away from the competition.

**Departure Message:** "Love you ALL! Believe in yourselves more than I believe in me you've got in the bag - Love you long time xoxo STW"

## QUEEN PROFILE: SUM TING WONG

Sum Ting Wong, whose real name is Bo Zeng, is a talented drag queen hailing from Birmingham. Bo Zeng was born in

Birmingham to Vietnamese immigrant parents of Chinese descent, adding a rich cultural background to her persona.

The name Sum Ting Wong holds a significant story behind it. In 2013, a news station in San Francisco, KTVU, mistakenly aired gag names that sounded stereotypically Chinese as the pilots of Asiana Airlines Flight 214. Among those names was "Sum Ting Wong," which humorously translates to "something wrong." Alongside other names like "Wi Tu Lo" (we [are] too low) and "Ho Lee Fuk" (holy fuck), it sparked controversy and outrage. Sum Ting Wong decided to reclaim and repurpose the name as her own, embracing it as a symbol of her British Vietnamese heritage.

Beyond her appearances on Drag Race, Sum Ting Wong has a presence on Twitch as a streamer and a musician, showcasing her talents in different creative realms.

## GUEST JUDGE PROFILE: GERI HORNER

Geraldine Estelle Horner, previously known as Geri Halliwell (born 6th of August 1972), is an accomplished English singer, songwriter, author, and actress. She gained fame in the 1990s as Ginger Spice, a prominent member of the globally successful girl group the Spice Girls. With over 100 million records sold worldwide, the Spice Girls hold the distinction of being the best-selling female group of all time. Halliwell, often associated with the group's empowering slogan "girl power," became a prominent figure, and her iconic Union Jack dress from the 1997 Brit Awards remains an enduring symbol.

In 1998, Halliwell made the decision to depart from the Spice Girls due to exhaustion and creative differences, but she rejoined the group when they reunited in 2007. Prior to her solo career, she released her debut album "Schizophonic" in 1999, which spawned several chart-topping singles in the UK, including

"Mi Chico Latino," "Lift Me Up," and "Bag It Up." Her solo success continued with her second album, "Scream If You Wanna Go Faster" in 2001, featuring the smash hit "It's Raining Men." She also released her third album, "Passion," in 2005, preceded by the single "Ride It."

Halliwell's talent and charismatic personality led to various opportunities beyond her music career. She served as a guest judge on the seventh and ninth series of The X Factor UK in 2010 and 2012, respectively. In 2013, she took on the role of a judge in the seventh series of Australia's Got Talent. Additionally, Halliwell ventured into writing, publishing two autobiographies, including "If Only" in 1999, and a series of children's novels titled "Ugenia Lavender." She has also dabbled in acting, appearing in films such as "Spice World" (1997), "Fat Slags: The Film" (2004), "Crank: High Voltage" (2009), and "The Crown with a Shadow" (2021) and "Gran Turismo," (2023)

Halliwell grew up in North Watford on a council estate and attended Watford Grammar School for Girls and Camden School for Girls. Before her music career, she worked as a nightclub dancer in Majorca, a presenter on the Turkish version of "Let's Make a Deal," and a glamour model. At 19, she became a Page 3 girl in The Sun, a British tabloid newspaper. Following her rise to fame, nude photos of Halliwell were republished in various magazines, including Playboy and Penthouse, in 1998.

Halliwell's journey in the music industry began in 1994 when she responded to an advertisement in The Stage magazine along with Melanie C, Mel B, and Victoria Beckham. After a few line-up changes, the group, along with Emma Bunton, eventually formed the Spice Girls under the management of Simon Fuller. They signed with Virgin Records in September 1995 and gained immense popularity with their debut single "Wannabe" in 1996, which became a global hit. The Spice Girls achieved phenomenal success with a string of number-one singles and albums. Halliwell's vibrant personality and fiery red hair earned her the nickname "Ginger Spice."

The phrase "girl power," closely associated with Halliwell, became a defining slogan for the Spice Girls. In a 1996 interview with The Spectator magazine, Halliwell controversially mentioned former Prime Minister Margaret Thatcher as an inspiration for their ideology of girl power. She later clarified in a 2019 interview that girl power represents equality between genders and celebrates individuality and gender equality for everyone, regardless of labels.

Halliwell's portrayal of girl power and her friendship with George Michael were parodied in the BBC comedy series "Rock Profile." She was humorously depicted as a patronizing individual who stalks Michael and has delusions of marrying him. According to the portrayal, everything for Halliwell is "Girl Power."

## EPISODE FIVE: "GIRL GROUPS BATTLE ROYALE"

In this week's mini-challenge, the queens engage in a reading session, taking playful jabs at each other. Crystal emerges as the winner of the mini-challenge. For the maxi challenge, the queens are tasked with collaborating in teams to write original lyrics and perform to the song "Break Up (Bye Bye)."

Team 1 comprises Baga Chipz, Blu Hydrangea, and Divina De Campo, who form **"The Frock Destroyers."** Team 2 consists of Cheryl Hole, Crystal, and The Vivienne, forming **"Filth Harmony."**

On the runway, the theme is "Day at the Races." "The Frock Destroyers" are declared the winning team, with Baga Chipz, Blu Hydrangea, and Divina De Campo all securing victories in the challenge. Unfortunately, "Filth Harmony" is deemed the losing team. Cheryl Hole is declared safe, while Crystal and The Vivienne find themselves in the bottom two. They face off in a lip-sync battle, performing to the song "Power" by Little Mix. The Vivienne emerges victorious in the lip sync, while Crystal sashays away from the competition.

**Departure Message:** "YOU'RE A BUNCH OF UGLY, TALENTLESS LITTLE WITCHES – I'M GOING TO MISS YOU!! X"

## QUEEN PROFILE: CRYSTAL

Crystal, whose real name is Colin Munro, is a Canadian-British drag performer and TV host.

Originally from Newfoundland and raised in Nova Scotia, they attended university for costume design, as mentioned in their podcast.

In the late 2000s, Crystal relocated to London, England, initially working as an aerial performer in the circus before venturing into drag performance. They initially went by the drag name Crystal Beth, a play on crystal meth, but later decided to be known simply as Crystal. This change was made before their appearance on Drag Race UK to avoid making light of the serious issue of drug addiction. Crystal explained that they always wanted to be known by a single name but initially thought that having two names was a requirement in the drag scene. Within London's drag community, Crystal was renowned for their involvement in Mariah and Friendz, a regular drag night inspired by Mariah Carey, characterized by "delusion, bad fashion, and lip-sync malfunctions."

On Drag Race UK, Crystal finished in sixth place, eliminated during the "Girl Group Battle Royale" challenge after a lip-sync against eventual winner The Vivienne.

Since their Drag Race UK stint, Crystal has made appearances as a special guest on Canada's Drag Race, participating in the "Star Sixty-Nine" episode as a caller for a psychic hotline mini-challenge. They also secured hosting duties on Group Sext, an LGBTQ dating reality show with a social distancing theme, airing on OutTV. Crystal additionally served as a drag mentor in the competition series Call Me Mother.

## GUEST JUDGE PROFILE: JADE THIRLWALL

Jade Amelia Thirlwall (born on 26th December 1992) is an English singer and songwriter known for her time as a member of the English girl group Little Mix. She gained prominence in the 2010s as part of the group, which achieved numerous chart successes, including nineteen top-ten singles, five number-ones, and six top-five studio albums on the UK Albums Chart. Little Mix made history as the first girl group to accomplish these milestones and spent a total of 100 weeks within the top 10 of the UK Singles

Chart. In 2022, Thirlwall signed a recording contract with RCA Records, embarking on a solo career following the group's hiatus.

Aside from her work with Little Mix, Thirlwall is also a talented songwriter and signed a publishing deal with Sony/ATV Music in 2019. She has collaborated on songs for various artists, including Twice, Billy Porter, Britney Spears, Iggy Azalea, and Nayeon. Beyond her contributions to the music industry, Thirlwall is an ambassador for Stonewall and actively engages in political and social activism. She advocates for LGBTQ+ rights, supports a ban on transgender conversion therapy in the UK, promotes the Black Lives Matter movement, and is involved in various charitable endeavours. In recognition of her activism, she received the Gay Times Honour for Allyship in 2021.

Thirlwall was born in South Shields, Tyne and Wear, England, to parents Norma Badwi and James Thirlwall. She has an older brother named Karl. Her heritage includes Egyptian and Yemeni ancestry from her mother's side and English descent from her father's side. Thirlwall identifies as mixed-race and has been actively reconnecting with her Arab-Egyptian-Yemeni heritage, including learning the language, with the goal of exploring the Middle East further.

Her journey in the music industry began when she auditioned for The X Factor UK in 2008 at the age of 15, but was eliminated during the boot-camp stage. She returned in 2010 but failed. Finally, in 2011 at the age of 18, Thirlwall auditioned again and advanced to the bootcamp stage. She joined forces with Leigh-Anne Pinnock, Perrie Edwards, and Jesy Nelson to form the group initially known as Rhythmix. After going through various challenges, the group eventually became Little Mix and went on to win The X Factor, making history as the first girl group to win the show.

As a member of Little Mix, Thirlwall contributed to the group's success by co-writing over 50 songs, including their UK number-one singles "Wings" in 2012 and "Shout Out to My Ex" in 2016. Little Mix has been credited with revitalizing the girl band genre in the UK and has become one of the country's best-selling acts. In December 2021, the group announced a hiatus to pursue solo projects.

Since embarking on her solo career, Thirlwall has appeared on RuPaul's Drag Race and made her acting debut in the British musical television drama series Mood. She signed a recording contract with RCA Records in the UK and USA and has engaged in various collaborations and projects. Thirlwall's artistry blends pop, R&B, and dance-pop, drawing influences from genres such as tropical house, Latin pop, and electronic music. She grew up listening to Motown and has a deep appreciation for Drag Culture, Drag Queens, and artists like RuPaul.

# EPISODE SIX: "THIRSTY WERK"

In this week's exciting mini-challenge, the queens engage in a playful game called Boxers, Briefs, or Commando, accompanied by the alluring pit crew. Ultimately, it is the fabulous Divina De Campo who emerges victorious, showcasing her wit and charm.

Moving on to the maxi challenge, the queens are tasked with an intriguing endeavour: campaigning, marketing, and creating their very own brand of bottled water. With their creativity and business acumen put to the test, the queens dive into the challenge with enthusiasm and determination.

As the runway segment unfolds, the queens grace the stage with their Rainy Day Eleganza looks, exuding elegance and style. Divina De Campo and The Vivienne impress the judges, receiving positive critiques for their impeccable presentations. Ultimately, it is The Vivienne who secures the win, earning recognition for her outstanding performance.

Meanwhile, Baga Chipz finds herself in a safe position, receiving mixed feedback from the judges. On the other hand, Blu Hydrangea and Cheryl Hole face more critical assessments. Unfortunately, Blu's journey on the show comes to an end as she faces off against Cheryl in an electrifying lip-sync battle. With the dynamic tune of "Call My Name (Wideboys Remix)" by Cheryl setting the stage on fire, Cheryl Hole delivers a stunning performance, earning her victory in the lip-sync. Blu Hydrangea gracefully sashays away, leaving a memorable impression on the competition.

**Departure Message:** "Not just a look Queen! BLU came, BLU slayed, BLU conquered for N.I. Love you ALL! BLU Hydrangea "

## QUEEN PROFILE: BLU HYDRANGEA

Blu Hydrangea, born Joshua Cargill on 15th of February 1996, is a talented drag queen hailing from Belfast, Northern Ireland. They rose to prominence as a contestant on the first season of RuPaul's Drag Race UK in 2019 and later competed on RuPaul's Drag Race: UK vs the World in 2022.

Blu Hydrangea's career took off when they were announced as a cast member of RuPaul's Drag Race UK in September 2019. Despite their undeniable talent, they finished in fifth place on the series, ultimately being eliminated after losing the lip-sync against fellow contestant Cheryl Hole.

Beyond the Drag Race franchise, Blu Hydrangea has made a name for themselves as a renowned makeup artist. They are also part of the sensational band known as the Frock Destroyers, alongside Baga Chipz and Divina de Campo. In addition, Blu and their fellow queens host the BBC web series called Strictly Frocked Up. This weekly show features them reviewing each episode of Strictly Come Dancing.

In January 2022, Blu Hydrangea was announced as one of the contestants for RuPaul's Drag Race: UK vs the World. In their personal life, Blu Hydrangea grew up in Royal Hillsborough before relocating to Belfast. In a March 2022 interview, they openly identified as non-binary, highlighting their unique and authentic self-expression.

## GUEST JUDGE PROFILE: CHERYL

Cheryl Ann Tweedy, born on the 30th of June 1983, is an English singer and TV personality. Cheryl was born and raised in Newcastle upon Tyne. She grew up in the suburbs of Walker and Heaton, showing an interest in dancing from a young age and participated in dance recitals on various television shows in the UK.

She gained fame in 2002 as a member of Girls Aloud, a girl group formed on ITV's Popstars: The Rivals, which went on to achieve tremendous success. The group's debut single, "Sound of the Underground," became the 2002 Christmas number one in the UK. Girls Aloud released several successful albums and singles, earning them numerous awards and accolades.

Girls Aloud's musical style primarily encompasses pop, although they ventured into various genres such as electropop, dance-pop, and dance-rock throughout their career. Their collaborations with Brian Higgins and his songwriting and production team Xenomania garnered widespread acclaim, as they brought an innovative approach to mainstream pop music. Remarkably, Girls Aloud achieved sustained success, becoming one of the few UK reality television acts to amass a fortune of £30 million by May 2010. In the 2007 edition of Guinness World Records, they were recognised as the "Most Successful Reality TV Group." The group also holds the record for the "Most Consecutive Top Ten Entries in the UK by a Female Group" in the 2008 edition and reclaimed the title of "Most Successful Reality TV Group" in the 2011 edition. Additionally, Girls Aloud has been acknowledged as the biggest-selling girl group of the 21st century in the United Kingdom, with over 4.3 million singles sold and 4 million albums sold in the UK alone. Girls Aloud disbanded in March 2013.

Cheryl launched a successful solo career in 2009, releasing four studio albums: "3 Words" (2009), "Messy Little Raindrops" (2010), "A Million Lights" (2012), and "Only Human" (2014). These albums produced several hit singles, including five number-one songs on the UK Singles Chart, making Cheryl the first British female solo artist to achieve this. However, her record was surpassed by Jess Glynne in 2018.

Cheryl took on the role of a judge in the UK version of The X Factor in 2008, where she gained recognition for her exceptional mentoring abilities (she mentored the winners of series five and six, Alexandra Burke and Joe McElderry, respectively). Cheryl later ventured into the American edition of the show, although her tenure was relatively brief. From 2019 to 2020, Cheryl served as a judge on The Greatest Dancer. In 2023, she made her stage debut in the West End play "2:22 A Ghost Story."

Known for her fashion sense, Cheryl has been recognised as a style icon and has graced the covers of British Vogue, Elle, and Harper's Bazaar. She was also the face of L'Oréal cosmetics from 2009 to 2018. As of October 2014, her net worth was estimated to be £20 million. Cheryl's personal life has also been in the public eye. She was married to footballer Ashley Cole from 2006 to 2010. She has been involved in charitable work, including establishing The Cheryl Cole Foundation.

## EPISODE SEVEN: "FAMILY THAT DRAGS TOGETHER"

In this week's mini-challenge, the queens engage in a lively puppet showdown. Divina De Campo emerges as the winner of the mini-challenge. As for the main challenge, the queens are tasked with giving a drag makeover to a member of their own family.

During the runway presentation, Divina De Campo and The Vivienne received commendations from the judges, with Divina ultimately securing the victory for the challenge. Unfortunately, Baga Chipz and Cheryl Hole face negative critiques and find themselves in the bottom two. To determine their fate, they perform a lip-sync to the soulful tune "Tears Dry on Their Own" by Amy Winehouse. Baga Chipz delivers an exceptional performance, leading to her victory in the lip sync, while Cheryl Hole must bid her farewell and sashay away from the competition.

**Departure Message:** "I'm all gamed out! You're finally getting rid of me! Kill it top 3 – So Proud! May the best GIRL win XOXO Cheryl Hole "

## QUEEN PROFILE: CHERYL HOLE

Cheryl Hole, born on 18 October 1993 as Luke Underwood-Bleach, is an English drag queen hailing from Chelmsford, Essex. She gained recognition as one of the initial contestants on RuPaul's Drag Race UK in 2019 and later competed in the inaugural season of RuPaul's Drag Race: UK vs the World in 2022. Cheryl's drag persona pays homage to former Girls Aloud singer Cheryl Cole.

Career-wise, Cheryl Hole and her fiancé Haydn appeared on the Comedy Central show Your Face Or Mine? Hosted by Jimmy Carr and Katherine Ryan on 3rd of April 2019. On 21st of August 2019, she was announced as one of the ten queens participating in the first series of RuPaul's Drag Race UK.

Following her Drag Race UK journey, Cheryl Hole joined the cast of series one for a 12-gig UK tour in November 2019, hosted by Drag Race alum Alyssa Edwards. In December 2019, she served as Virgin Media's Christmas 'fairy gift mother' for their Christmas campaign, surprising and gifting Virgin Media customers. In July 2020, Cheryl started her podcast called Girl Group Gossip, produced by World of Wonder, where she discusses various topics with a co-host and a special guest.

In November 2020, Cheryl Hole teamed up with Drag Race UK series 1 winner The Vivienne for three consecutive episodes of the UK version of the Netflix YouTube series I Like to Watch. On the 24th of September 2021, Cheryl Hole and her partner Haydn tied the knot, resulting in their last names becoming Underwood-Bleach. In 2022, Cheryl Hole made her West End debut in the play Death Drop.

## GUEST JUDGE PROFILE: MICHAELA COEL

Michaela Ewuraba Boakye-Collinson, professionally known as Michaela Coel, is a Ghanaian-British actress, filmmaker, singer, and composer. Born on 1st of October 1987 in East London to Ghanaian parents, Coel and her sister were raised by their mother primarily in Hackney and Tower Hamlets. She attended Catholic schools in East London, and she has spoken about her experience as the only black pupil in her age group, which led to her feeling isolated and bullying other students during her primary school years. However, her secondary education at a comprehensive school was different, and she didn't experience the same isolation.

Coel pursued higher education at the University of Birmingham from 2007 to 2009, studying English Literature and Theology. During this time, she participated in a masterclass with Ché Walker, an actor, playwright, and director, whom she met at open mic nights. In 2009, she transferred to the Guildhall School of Music and Drama, becoming the first black woman to enrol in five years. She received the Laurence Olivier Bursary Award, which supported her studies. Coel engaged in additional workshops and courses, such as the Mark Proulx workshop at Prima del Teatro and the Kat Francois Poetry Course at the Theatre Royal Stratford East. She completed her studies at the Guildhall School of Music and Drama in 2012.

Coel's journey in the entertainment industry began in 2006 when she started performing at poetry open mics in Ealing. Encouraged by Ché Walker, she applied to Guildhall after he saw her perform at the Hackney Empire. Coel's poetry performances took her to various notable stages, including Wembley Arena, Bush Theatre, Nuyorican Poets Cafe, and De Doelen in Rotterdam. During this time, she went by the name Michaela The Poet.

In 2009, Coel joined the Talawa Theatre Company summer school program called TYPT. She participated in the TYPT 2009 production of Krunch, directed by Amani Naphtali. She also released an album titled Fixing Barbie in the same year, showcasing her work as a poet and musician.

She gained prominence as the creator and star of the E4 sitcom Chewing Gum (2015–2017), for which she received a BAFTA Award for Best Female Comedy Performance. Coel's career continued to flourish as she appeared in BBC One drama London Spy in 2015 and played Lilyhot in the E4 sci-fi comedy-drama The Aliens the following year. Chewing Gum returned for a second series in January 2017. She also made appearances in Charlie Brooker's series Black Mirror in the episodes "Nosedive" and "USS Callister." Additionally, Coel had a minor role in the 2017 film Star Wars: The Last Jedi.

Coel's most significant critical success came with the creation, writing, production, co-direction, and starring role in the comedy-drama series I May Destroy You. Inspired by her personal experience of sexual assault, the show premiered on BBC One in the UK and HBO in the US in June 2020, receiving widespread acclaim. Coel declined a $1 million offer from Netflix after they refused to grant her ownership of the show's intellectual property. Her work on I May Destroy You earned her numerous accolades, including the British Academy Television Award for Best Actress. She was included in Time's 100 Most Influential People in 2020 and was recognised as one of the breakout stars of 2020 in film. Coel's influential presence also led to her inclusion in British Vogue's list of influential women in 2020. She ranked fourth on the Powerlist of the most influential people of African or African-Caribbean heritage in the United Kingdom for her impact through I May Destroy You.

Coel portrayed Kate Ashby in the series Black Earth Rising (2018) and Simone in the film Been So Long (2018). In July 2021, Coel was cast in the film Black Panther: Wakanda Forever, where she portrays the character Aneka, a member of the Dora Milaje.

Aside from her successful career, Coel published her first book, Misfits: A Personal Manifesto, in September 2021. The book, based on her MacTaggart lecture at the 2018 Edinburgh Festival, explores her experiences with racism and misogyny and serves as a powerful manifesto on embracing one's truth and celebrating differences.

Coel has showcased her cultural heritage on the red carpet, wearing a dress made of Kente cloth designed by her mother at the 2016 British Academy Television Awards. She has discussed her religious background, initially embracing Pentecostalism and celibacy, similar to her Chewing Gum character Tracey. However, she stopped practising Pentecostalism after attending Guildhall. Coel has also identified as aromantic.

## EPISODE EIGHT: "GRAND FINALE"

In the last stage of the season's ultimate challenge, the competing queens are tasked with writing, recording, and performing their own verses to RuPaul's hit song "Rock It (To The Moon)." As the tension builds, the queens showcase their final runway looks, making a memorable last impression. The excitement reaches its peak as all the previously eliminated queens return to join the grand finale.

With all the queens gathered, RuPaul delivers the news that Baga Chipz has been eliminated, narrowing down the competition to the final two contenders: Divina De Campo and The Vivienne. The atmosphere electrifies as these talented queens prepare for a thrilling lip-sync battle to the iconic tune "I'm Your Man" by Wham!

After an intense performance, RuPaul makes the momentous announcement, and The Vivienne is crowned the ultimate winner of the season, a testament to her outstanding talent and charisma. Divina De Campo, having displayed incredible artistry and skill, earns the honourable position of runner-up. It's a bittersweet ending as the journey comes to a close, but the legacy of these queens will forever shine in the world of drag.

## QUEEN PROFILE: BAGA CHIPZ

Leo Loren, professionally known as Baga Chipz, is an acclaimed English drag queen who gained prominence through her appearances RuPaul's Drag Race and RuPaul's Drag Race: UK vs the World.

As a member of "The Buffalo Girls," a renowned drag troupe featuring Lady Lloyd and Silver Summers, Baga Chipz has been part of a dynamic and talented ensemble. Her journey into the spotlight gained momentum in 2014 when she appeared on Drag Queens of London, a captivating series that delved into the lives of drag queens both on and off the stage.

The breakthrough moment for Baga Chipz came in August 2019 when she was announced as one of the ten queens competing in the inaugural season of RuPaul's Drag Race UK. Throughout the competition, she showcased her exceptional skills and won three challenges, ultimately finishing in a commendable third place. Following her Drag Race journey, Baga Chipz embarked on a tour with her fellow season one contestants, hosted by Drag Race alumna Alyssa Edwards. She also made an appearance at the first-ever RuPaul's DragCon UK in January 2020, cementing her status as a fan favourite.

In December 2019, Baga Chipz teamed up with fellow RuPaul's Drag Race UK contestant The Vivienne for the show Morning T&T on WOW Presents Plus. The duo reprised their memorable Snatch Game impersonations of Donald Trump and Margaret Thatcher, respectively, hosting a fictional television news show. The success of the series led to additional episodes, including a special one filmed at DragCon UK. Notable guests on the show included other Drag Race UK alumni, such as Sum Ting Wong and Cheryl Hole, who portrayed Queen Elizabeth II and Gemma Collins, respectively.

Continuing to explore her creative activities, Baga Chipz joined forces with The Vivienne in March 2020 to present the UK version of I Like to Watch, a popular web series produced by Netflix where they provide entertaining reviews of Netflix programming.

Outside the realm of drag, Baga Chipz showcased her culinary skills on Celebrity Masterchef in July 2020, displaying her versatility and ability to thrive in diverse environments. In September 2020, she released her debut single titled "When The

Sun Goes Down" in collaboration with Saara Aalto. Baga Chipz also made appearances on the ITV series Celebrity Karaoke Club and secured a role in the Channel 4 school drama series Ackley Bridge in 2021, appearing in the fifth series in 2022.

Baga Chipz returned to compete on RuPaul's Drag Race: UK vs. the World, facing off against drag queens from various iterations of the Drag Race franchise. While she showcased her talent and secured a spot in the finale, she ultimately tied for third place with fellow competitor Jujubee, losing her lip-sync against season runner-up Mo Heart in the first round of the finale Lip-Sync for the Crown tournament.

With her vibrant personality, captivating performances, and unwavering charm, Baga Chipz has left an indelible mark on the world of drag and continues to inspire audiences worldwide.

## RUNNER UP: DIVINA DE CAMPO

Owen Richard Farrow, professionally known as Divina de Campo, is a talented English drag queen, singer, and actor. During their formative years, Farrow faced challenges with their sexuality and experienced difficulties in school. However, after completing their university degree, they found support and encouragement from their husband, who urged them to explore the world of drag.

Farrow's captivating journey in drag began in 2005, adopting the stage name Divina de Campo, which is inspired by the iconic Divine, an individual who served as a significant source of inspiration for them. They regularly showcased their talent at Kiki, a renowned venue in Manchester's Gay Village, until its closure in 2020.

In January 2016, de Campo took a leap onto a different stage, auditioning for the popular television show The Voice. Their performance of "Poor Wandering One" from The Pirates of Penzance caught the attention of the judges, including their idol, Boy George. Although none of the judges turned their chairs during the audition, Boy George later expressed regret for not selecting de Campo. Demonstrating their versatility, de Campo took on the role of a performer in the play The Ruby Slippers in December 2016, which delved into themes of identity and prejudice within the LGBTQ+ community.

De Campo's involvement in the community extended beyond their performances. In 2017, they participated in a campaign supporting the George House Trust, a charity dedicated to assisting individuals living with HIV. They also hosted Superbia's Drag Queen Story Time in December 2017, sharing the joy of storytelling with young children. In 2018, de Campo served as a judge on the show All Together Now, showcasing their expertise and contributing to the vibrant world of entertainment. Their involvement continued with a role in the musical Dancing Bear, exploring themes of faith, sexuality, and gender identity in February 2018.

The transformative moment in de Campo's career arrived on 21st of August 2019 when they were announced as one of the ten queens competing in the first season of RuPaul's Drag Race UK. This opportunity allowed de Campo to display their exceptional talent, winning three challenges and earning the honourable position of first runner-up. They embarked on a UK tour alongside their fellow season one contestants from November to December 2019, hosted by the esteemed Drag Race alumna Alyssa Edwards. De Campo solidified their rising star status by attending the inaugural RuPaul's DragCon UK in January 2020, engaging with fans and leaving a lasting impact on the drag community.

In 2020, de Campo headlined at Portsmouth Pride, thrilling audiences with their captivating performances at Castlefield, Southsea. As the world faced the challenges of the COVID-19 pandemic, de Campo embraced the virtual realm. They became a featured cast member in the first-ever Digital Drag Fest, an online festival providing interactive experiences, tips, and prizes for attendees of all ages. They continued their digital journey, participating in the second annual Digital Drag Fest in May 2021 while also representing Australia in the Isolation Song Contest.

De Campo continued to flourish as they took part in Turn On Fest, a virtual LGBTQ+ performing arts festival based in Manchester, in March 2021. In April, they graced the digital revival of The Importance of Being Earnest, presented by Dukes Lancaster and the Lawrence Batley Theatre. May brought an opportunity for de Campo to shine as a featured performer in The Parking Lot Social Easter Panto, a unique drive-in show experience.

Adding to their impressive resume, de Campo secured the role of Mary Sunshine in the 2021/2022 UK Tour of the beloved musical Chicago, showcasing their exceptional talents to a broader audience. In May 2022, they lent their voice to the character Popcorn Reilly in Alaska's Drag: The Musical, a studio recording of a theatrical production that delves into the story of two rival drag bars facing financial struggles.

The recognition and accolades continued to pour in for de Campo, as they were honoured with the Best Performance in a Musical award at the UK Theatre Awards in October 2022 for their outstanding portrayal in Hedwig and the Angry Inch, a co-production by Leeds Playhouse and HOME. With their immense talent, powerful performances, and dedication to their craft,

Divina de Campo has become a celebrated figure in the world of drag, captivating audiences with their extraordinary presence.

## SERIES ONE WINNER: THE VIVIENNE

James Lee Williams, known professionally as The Vivienne, is a prominent Welsh drag queen, born and raised in North Wales before relocating to Liverpool at the age of 16.

The Vivienne gained recognition as the first UK RuPaul's Drag Race ambassador in 2015 and went on to win the opening season of RuPaul's Drag Race UK in 2019. In 2022, she returned to compete in the seventh season of RuPaul's Drag Race All Stars.

As part of her victory on Drag Race UK, The Vivienne was granted her own online television series, later titled The Vivienne Takes on Hollywood. The series, which premiered on 9th of April 2020 on BBC Three, follows her journey to Hollywood to produce her own music video, showcasing her talent and creativity.

The Vivienne's name choice was influenced by her affinity for Vivienne Westwood clothing, and she added the definite article to make it unique. She has performed in various Liverpool bars, including Superstar Boudoir, GBar, and Heaven, establishing herself as a prominent figure in the local drag scene.

Her participation in RuPaul's Drag Race UK was announced on the 21st of August 2019, quickly becoming a fan favourite. In addition to her drag performances, The Vivienne actively supports charitable causes. She participated in Jag Race, a racing competition in collaboration with Jaguar Cars, to raise funds for Sahir House, a Liverpool-based charity that provides support for individuals affected by HIV.

Following her victory on RuPaul's Drag Race UK, The Vivienne embarked on a tour with the cast of the show, showcasing her talent to audiences across the UK. She also starred in the web series Morning T&T alongside fellow Drag Race UK contestant Baga Chipz, where they humorously hosted a fictional television news show using their iconic Snatch Game impersonations.

In March 2020, The Vivienne embarked on her own adventure with the six-part series The Vivienne Takes on Hollywood. The show documented her journey to Los Angeles to create a music video and was simultaneously streamed on WOW Presents Plus and aired on BBC Three. She also co-hosted the UK version of I Like to Watch, a web series produced by Netflix, where she and Baga Chipz provided humorous reviews of Netflix programming.

The Vivienne's talent extends beyond drag, as she voiced the character of Donald Trump in the BBC Three documentary Trump in Tweets. She also made a guest appearance as herself in the popular ITV soap opera Emmerdale in June 2021. In January 2022, she participated in Channel 4's Celebrity Hunted, raising funds for Stand Up to Cancer.

In April 2022, The Vivienne was announced as a contestant on the seventh season of RuPaul's Drag Race All Stars, competing against other previous winners for the prestigious title of "Queen of All Queens." Additionally, she made history as the first drag artist to participate in the fifteenth series of the ITV ice-skating reality show, Dancing on Ice, which was announced in October 2022.

The contestants from Series One were later announced to star in a documentary web television series that would follow their tour after the conclusion of the first season of RuPaul's Drag Race UK. The series premiered internationally on 10th of September 2020, on WOW Presents Plus, and made its debut on BBC iPlayer on the 15th of November 2020.

The documentary series, titled "God Shave the Queens," featured the Season one contestants of RuPaul's Drag Race UK, along with Alyssa Edwards from Season 5 of the American version, who served as the host for the six-city tour across the UK—the first season of RuPaul's Drag Race UK garnered significant success, leading to the creation of numerous memes, receiving critical acclaim, receiving multiple award nominations, and even achieving chart success with a top ten single. The series proved to be a triumph for BBC Three, amassing a staggering 15.6 million requests on iPlayer thus far.

| Contestant | Age | Hometown | Result |
|---|---|---|---|
| The Vivienne | 26 | Liverpool, England | Winner |
| Divina de Campo | 35 | Brighouse, England | Runner-up |
| Baga Chipz | 29 | East London, England | 3rd place |
| Cheryl Hole | 25 | Chelmsford, England | 4th place |
| Blu Hydrangea | 23 | Belfast, Northern Ireland | 5th place |
| Crystal | 34 | East London, England | 6th place |
| Sum Ting Wong | 30 | Birmingham, England | 7th place |
| Vinegar Strokes | 34 | North London, England | 8th place |
| Scaredy Kat | 19 | Cricklade, England | 9th place |
| Gothy Kendoll | 21 | Leicester, England | 10th place |

*Information correct at time of filming*

# RUPAUL'S DRAG RACE UK SERIES 2

The second series of RuPaul's Drag Race UK was officially confirmed, and casting closed on 15th of November 2019. However, due to the COVID-19 pandemic, filming was indefinitely suspended. In June 2020, Michelle Visage, one of the show's judges, confirmed that production would resume once government guidelines permitted. She expressed excitement about the show's return, stating that they could not film in quarantine and would provide more information once the guidelines were lifted.

On 29th of October 2020, Alan Carr, another judge on the show, revealed during an interview on Lorraine that production had resumed, and he was set to resume filming the second series within two weeks. Carr mentioned that both RuPaul and Visage, who oversee the application auditions, had received more than double the number of applicants compared to the first series. He also mentioned that the show's secrecy extended to the judges, as they were not aware of which queens were still in the competition or who the guest judges would be until they arrived on set. Carr expressed his excitement, comparing his anticipation to that of a child waiting for an event like in an Alton Towers advert.

During an interview on The Graham Norton Show, guest judge Dawn French revealed herself as the first guest judge for the second series. She explained that the panel had been arranged to ensure social distancing, with each judge sitting at their own smaller panel rather than being seated together. French also shared that the BBC had originally approached her to be a full-time judge for the first series, but she had declined due to not living in London and the extensive travel it would entail.

In November 2020, the BBC announced that the second series would air in early 2021. A BBC spokesperson stated that the upcoming series would be even bigger than the first, featuring twelve queens competing for the title of the UK's Next Drag Superstar over ten weeks. RuPaul himself expressed his anticipation for the return of the show, stating that season two would bring the hope, joy, laughter, and glitter that fans had come to expect from the brilliant queens. Additionally, the casting process for season three was underway to showcase the best talent Great Britain had to offer.

The second series of RuPaul's Drag Race UK premiered on the 14th of January 2021.

## EPISODE ONE: "ROYALTY RETURNS"

In the premiere episode of the show, the queens make their grand entrance into the workroom, ready to embark on their first challenge: a glamorous tennis photoshoot. Following that, they gear up to showcase their runway skills by serving two distinct looks. The judging panel, consisting of the fabulous Michelle Visage, the witty Graham Norton, and the esteemed actress and fashion icon Elizabeth Hurley, offers their critiques.

Unfortunately, one queen must bid farewell as they sashay away from the competition. Asttina Mandella, Ellie Diamond, and Lawrence Chaney impressed the judges with their exceptional performances, with Asttina Mandella ultimately securing victory in the challenge. However, Bimini Bon Boulash, Joe Black, and Sister Sister receive less favourable feedback, leading to Bimini and Joe engaging in a lip sync battle, with Joe eventually being eliminated.

**Departure Message:** "Auf wiedersehen you camp old bitches. Love you, see you soon JB"

# QUEEN PROFILE: JOE BLACK

Joseph Lewis Black, born on the 23rd of December 1989, is a renowned British musician and drag queen hailing from Brighton, England. With a career spanning since 2008, Black has established himself as a prominent figure in the captivating genre of dark cabaret drag. He frequently graces the stages of Brighton, his hometown, and is a regular performer at the esteemed Brighton Fringe festival. Known for his musical prowess, Black's performances feature his exceptional skills on instruments like the piano, accordion, musical saw, ukulele, and theremin. Over the past decade, he has embarked on extensive tours across the United Kingdom, Europe, Australia, and America, showcasing his talent and captivating audiences worldwide.

In December 2020, Black's participation in the highly anticipated second series of RuPaul's Drag Race UK was announced. Unfortunately, he faced elimination early on in a lip sync battle against fellow contestant Bimini Bon-Boulash, performing to "Relax" by Frankie Goes to Hollywood. However, in a surprising twist, Black made a triumphant return in episode five when the previously eliminated queens (excluding Ginny Lemon) were given the opportunity to re-enter the competition. Through the votes of the remaining contestants, he secured his place back in the race. However, his journey came to an end once again as he faced another lip sync challenge, this time against contestant Tia Kofi, with the song "Don't Leave Me This Way" by The Communards.

Following his elimination, Black announced exciting plans; he revealed a UK Tour named Decopunk, for September 2021, promising fans a captivating experience. Additionally, he unveiled a limited-edition gin of the same name, boasting an impressive 40% ABV. Furthermore, in February 2022, Black embarked on RuPaul's Drag Race UK: The Official Tour, joining the entire cast of the second series for an exhilarating showcase presented in collaboration with World of Wonder and promoter Voss Events.

Beyond his illustrious career, Black has shown remarkable courage and openness in discussing his personal life. He has spoken candidly about his experience living with and managing Tourette's Syndrome, providing inspiration to others facing similar challenges.

## GUEST JUDGE PROFILE: ELIZABETH HURLEY

Elizabeth Jane Hurley, born on 10th of June 1965, is an English actress and model. She has had a diverse career in both film and television.

In her early acting career, Hurley appeared in the film "Passenger 57" in 1992. Her breakthrough role came in 1997 when she portrayed Vanessa Kensington in the comedy film "Austin Powers: International Man of Mystery" and gained further recognition as the Devil in "Bedazzled" in 2000. She also appeared in the E! original series "The Royals" from 2015 to 2018 and played Morgan le Fay in "Runaways" in 2019, based on the Marvel Comics series.

Hurley's iconic moment in the media came in 1994 when she attended the London premiere of "Four Weddings and a Funeral" with Hugh Grant. She wore a revealing black Versace dress held together with gold safety pins, which garnered significant attention and media coverage.

As a model, Hurley has been associated with the cosmetics company Estée Lauder since 1995, when they gave her first modelling job at the age of 29. She has been featured in numerous campaigns and represented their products, particularly perfumes such as Sensuous, Intuition, and Pleasures. Additionally, Hurley owns her own beachwear line called Elizabeth Hurley Beach, which she launched in 2005.

In terms of her personal life, Hurley was born in Basingstoke, Hampshire, and attended Harriet Costello School. She developed an interest in punk fashion during her teenage years and enrolled in ballet classes. After studying dance and theatre at the London Studio Centre, she was expelled in 1986 for going AWOL to a Greek island.

Hurley has been involved in various charitable activities, supporting causes such as breast cancer research, The Prince's Trust, and the Elton John AIDS Foundation. She has also been active in politics, expressing support for the United Kingdom leaving the European Union in the 2016 referendum.

## EPISODE TWO: "RATS: THE RUSICAL"

After Joe Black's elimination, the queens gathered to discuss the events of the previous week's episode. The mini challenge required the contestants to form a Drag Race cabinet, with positions such as Secretary of Shade, Trade Minister, Leader of the House of Loading It Up, and Baroness Basic. A'Whora, Tayce, Lawrence Chaney, and Tia Kofi emerged as the winners in their respective categories.

For the main challenge, the contestants were tasked with performing in "Rats: The Rusical," receiving vocal coaching from Michelle Visage and choreography from Jay Revell and Kieran Daley Ward. On the main stage, they had to present a look based on the theme "Surprise, Surprise." A'Whora, Asttina Mandella, Bimini Bon-Boulash, Ginny Lemon, and Sister Sister were deemed safe, while Ellie Diamond, Tia Kofi, and Veronica Green received praise for their performances.

Cherry Valentine, Lawrence Chaney, and Tayce faced critiques, with Lawrence Chaney being spared from the lip-sync. Veronica Green emerged as the winner of the challenge, while Cherry Valentine and Tayce had to lip-sync for their lives to Elaine Paige's "Memory." Unfortunately, Cherry Valentine was eliminated from the competition.

**Departure Message:** "Always remember. Love yourself first. Can't wait to pop your cherries again! Love C"

## QUEEN PROFILE: CHERRY VALENTINE

George Ward, known by his stage name Cherry Valentine, was an English drag queen and mental health nurse, born on 30$^{th}$ of November 1993 in Darlington, County Durham, Ward was raised in an English Traveller community, and he proudly acknowledged his Romani heritage, making him the first contestant in the Drag Race franchise to do so. Ward's journey and background were explored in the BBC documentary film "Cherry Valentine: Gypsy Queen and Proud" and an episode of the documentary series "God Shave the Queens."

In his early life, Ward faced challenges growing up in a strict environment that did not accept drag. He bravely came out to his parents by writing them a letter before leaving home for a week. Although his parents individually spoke to him about it, they did not discuss his sexual orientation further. Ward later reflected on his upbringing, acknowledging the impact it had on his mental well-being. Despite the obstacles, Ward became the first member of his family to attend university, pursuing a degree in mental health nursing at the University of Cumbria, where he discovered and became involved in Manchester's vibrant drag scene.

Ward qualified as a mental health nurse in 2015 and began performing as Cherry Valentine in 2016, all while working in a children's psychiatric intensive-care unit and caring for adults with Huntington's disease. Choosing the name "Cherry Valentine" for his drag persona, Ward drew inspiration from cherry-scented bath wash and his grandmother's love for sherry while adding "Valentine" due to his fondness for Valentine's Day.

In December 2020, Cherry Valentine was announced as one of the twelve contestants on the second series of RuPaul's Drag Race UK. His experience as a nurse allowed him to understand and connect with people on a deeper level, which he believed was an asset in the drag world. Although Cherry Valentine did not impress the judges with his performance in the Rusical episode, he left a lasting impression on viewers with his fierce aesthetic and charismatic confessionals.

During the COVID-19 pandemic, when filming for the show was halted, Ward returned to work in the National Health Service (NHS) to provide relief efforts and assist with the UK's vaccine rollout. In the special episode "Queens on Lockdown," which delved into the contestants' lives during the pandemic, Cherry Valentine discussed his return to the NHS and the challenges faced during that time.

After his time on Drag Race UK, Cherry Valentine released dance-pop singles such as "Aesthetic" and "Iconic" in 2021, followed by "Stay Here Forever" in 2022. He also appeared in music videos for "My House" by Jodie Harsh and "Good Ones" by Charli XCX in 2021. Alongside other series contestants, Cherry Valentine embarked on RuPaul's Drag Race UK: The Official Tour in February 2022.

Cherry Valentine's story and journey were highlighted in the premiere episode of the documentary series "God Shave the Queens," which focused on the tour. Reflecting on his documentary "Cherry Valentine: Gypsy Queen and Proud," Ward returned to his Traveller community, which he had left at the age of 18. Despite initial fears and uncertainty about how to approach the film due to the lack of mainstream attention and education on LGBTQ+ Travellers, the documentary received widespread critical acclaim. Ward's openness about his Romani heritage paved the way for more contestants in the Drag Race franchise, such as series 1 winner The Vivienne, to acknowledge their Romani background.

On 18th of September 2022, at the age of 28, Ward tragically passed away in Hornsey, a district in North London. The coroner's inquest, held on the 9th of February 2023, determined that Ward's cause of death was suicide by hanging. The news of his death deeply saddened the Drag Race community, and numerous contestants from both series 2 of RuPaul's Drag Race UK and other seasons paid tribute to him. Asttina Mandella, A'Whora, Bimini Bon-Boulash, Ellie Diamond, Ginny Lemon, Joe Black, Lawrence Chaney, Sister Sister, Tayce, Tia Kofi, as well as Baga Chipz, Cheryl Hole, Priyanka, Sum Ting Wong, and The Vivienne all expressed their condolences and shared their memories of Ward.

RuPaul himself described Ward as a "bright star and a lovely person" who would forever remain in their hearts. Michelle Visage, a judge on Drag Race, fondly remembered Ward as someone who was "one of a kind with a laugh as big as his heart".

To honour Ward's memory, a special in memoriam segment was included in an episode of series 4 of Drag Race UK, and a GoFundMe campaign called Cherry's Legacy Fundraiser surpassed its goal of £10,000. Additionally, the organisers of RuPaul's DragCon UK announced that a condolence book would be dedicated to Cherry Valentine. In October 2022, Ward's production company, Throne Events, announced a memorial concert titled "Iconic: The Cherry Valentine Memorial Concert," which took place in November at Clapham Grand in London. Tickets to the concert were made available at no cost, with donations going towards Ward's legacy fund and mental health charities. The live-streamed event featured performances by Drag Race UK contestants Elektra Fence and Joe Black, as well as a performance by the group Traveller Pride. Attendees had the opportunity to pay their respects by scattering rose petals around Ward's entrance look from the show.

## GUEST JUDGE PROFILE: SHERIDAN SMITH

Sheridan Caroline Sian Smith OBE is an accomplished English actress, singer, and television personality. Born on 25th of June 1981, in Epworth, Lincolnshire. She discovered her passion for performing at a young age and studied dance at the Joyce Mason School of Dancing. She later attended South Axholme Comprehensive School and was a member of the National Youth Music Theatre. Smith continued her education at John Leggott College in Scunthorpe.

She gained recognition through her versatile roles in popular sitcoms such as "The Royle Family," "Two Pints of Lager and a Packet of Crisps," "Gavin & Stacey," and "Benidorm." Smith's talent extended to drama series, where she received critical acclaim for her performances in shows like "Jonathan Creek," "Mrs Biggs," "Cilla," "The C Word," "Black Work," and "The Moorside."

In addition to her television work, Smith has appeared in several feature films, including "Tower Block," "Quartet," and "The Huntsman: Winter's War." She has also showcased her singing abilities in various West End musicals like "Little Shop of Horrors," "Legally Blonde," "Funny Girl," and "Joseph and the Amazing Technicolour Dreamcoat." In 2017, she released her debut album, titled "Sheridan," followed by her second album, "A Northern Soul," in 2018.

Smith's talent extends to voice acting as well. In 2006, she began voicing the character Lucie Miller for the Doctor Who audio range produced by Big Finish. She also participated in the D-Day 75 tribute event, commemorating the 75th anniversary of the Normandy landings, where she performed the song "When the Lights Go On Again."

Throughout her career, Smith has received numerous accolades, including two Laurence Olivier Awards, a British Academy Television Award, a National Television Award, a BPG Award, and two International Emmy Award nominations. In recognition of her contributions to drama, she was appointed Officer of the Order of the British Empire (OBE) in the 2015 New Year Honours.

## EPISODE THREE: "WHO WORE IT BEST?"

In the opening mini-challenge of the episode, the queens were tasked with a limbo competition in quick drag. For the main challenge, the queens paired up with their drag sisters. The five teams had to create coordinated looks using matching colours and fabrics. The winners of the mini challenge, Tayce and Veronica Green, had the privilege of assigning the colours to the duos. A'Whora and Tayce were given black, Ginny Lemon and Sister Sister got pink, Tia Kofi and Veronica Green received green, Asttina Mandella and Bimini Bon-Boulash were assigned blue, and Ellie Diamond and Lawrence Chaney had gold.

While working on their looks, RuPaul revealed that within each duo, one queen would excel while the other would be at the bottom. On the main stage, A'Whora, Bimini Bon-Boulash, Lawrence Chaney, Sister Sister, and Veronica Green were praised for wearing their outfits best, with Lawrence Chaney ultimately winning the challenge. After the queens untucked in the workroom, Ellie Diamond and Tayce were declared safe. Ginny Lemon received some negative critiques but was deemed safe. Asttina Mandella and Tia Kofi found themselves in the bottom two and had to lip-sync for their lives to "Don't Start Now" by Dua Lipa. Unfortunately, Asttina Mandella was asked to sashay away from the competition.

**Departure Message:** "Rude. Always to remember to have RAT BITE FEVER. Love you all FOREVER + ALWAYS. Asttina"

## QUEEN PROFILE: ASTTINA MANDELLA

Aston Joshua, born 11th of February 1993, professionally known as Asttina Mandella, is a talented British drag queen and dancer hailing from East London.

Asttina Mandella began her journey as a drag queen in 2012, but prior to 2020, she was primarily known for her impressive skills as a dancer. She has honed her expertise in various dance styles, including ballet, tap dance, jazz, voguing, hip-hop, waacking, and street dance. Mandella has had the opportunity to showcase her dancing talents as a backup dancer for renowned artists such as Hercules & Love Affair, The Pussycat Dolls, Little Mix, and Kanye West.

The name Asttina Mandella is a clever fusion of her birth name, the iconic American singer Tina Turner, and the respected former President of South Africa and philanthropist Nelson Mandela. In December 2020, she was selected as one of twelve contestants to participate in the second series of RuPaul's Drag Race UK.

During her time on the show, Asttina Mandella entered the Werk Room as the eleventh contestant and introduced the now-famous catchphrase 'Rude!' She showcased her talent and determination by winning the first episode of the series and delivering strong performances in subsequent challenges. However, in episode three, she found herself at the bottom and faced elimination in a lip sync battle against fellow contestant Tia Kofi, with the song "Don't Start Now" by Dua Lipa.

In February 2022, Asttina Mandella embarked on RuPaul's Drag Race UK: The Official Tour, joining the entire cast of the show's second series in association with World of Wonder and promoter Voss Events. Additionally, in August 2021, she was featured as a performer in Klub Kids London Presents: NOIR: The Tour, a production that donated 25% of its proceeds to the Black Lives Matter movement.

Asttina Mandella currently resides in East London, and she has used her platform to shed light on the representation of Black Queer icons within the United Kingdom. Alongside fellow contestant Tayce, their conversation on the topic sparked important discussions and reached a wide audience, making a significant impact on raising awareness and understanding.

## GUEST JUDGE PROFILE: JOURDAN DUNN

Jourdan Sherise Dunn, born 3rd of August 1990 in Brent, London. Dunn grew up in Greenford with her mother; she attended Elthorne Park High School in Hanwell. Despite feeling self-conscious about her height and weight during her teenage years, she caught the attention of others who suggested she should pursue modelling. Initially unsure about the profession, shows like America's Next Top Model sparked her interest and provided her with a new perspective.

At the age of 15, in early 2006, while accompanying a friend at a London Primark, Dunn was scouted by an agent from Storm Management. By early 2007, she started gracing international runways, and in February 2008, she made history as the first black model to walk the Prada runway in over a decade. In April 2014, Dunn was announced as the new face of Maybelline New York, solidifying her status as an icon according to models.com in July 2014. She is widely regarded as one of the supermodels of her generation.

Dunn made her runway debut at 16 during the New York shows in autumn 2007, walking for prominent designers such as Marc Jacobs and Polo Ralph Lauren. She quickly gained prominence in the industry, appearing in British Vogue as a "new star" in 2007 and being recognised as one of the top 10 newcomers by Style.com in 2008. Throughout her career, she has walked for numerous renowned designers and often stood out as the only black model in shows, a disparity she later criticized.

In July 2008, Dunn graced the cover of the Vogue Italia issue dedicated to black models, shot by Steven Meisel. She has been featured on the covers of various editions of Vogue, Elle, W Magazine, Glamour, and more. Dunn has worked with prestigious brands such as Burberry, Yves Saint Laurent, Calvin Klein, Michael Kors, Victoria's Secret and appeared in campaigns for Rihanna's collections with River Island.

Besides her success in the fashion world, Dunn has been open about her personal life. She has a son named Riley, born in 2009. In February 2020, she got engaged to rapper Dion Hamilton.

Dunn's accomplishments have earned her several accolades. In November 2008, she was named "Model of the Year" at the British Fashion Awards. She won the same title again in 2015. Additionally, she received the "Inspiration Award" at the Glamour Women of the Year Awards in 2015 for her philanthropic work and advocacy for diversity in the modelling industry.

Dunn has made appearances in music videos for Beyoncé's songs "Yoncé" and "XO." She also hosts a cooking show called "Well Dunn" on Jay Z's Life+Times YouTube channel, where she collaborates with celebrity guest co-chefs.

# EPISODE FOUR: "MORNING GLORY"

In the latest episode of the show, the queens faced the Great British Fake-Off mini-challenge, where they had to present cakes as if they were their own creations. Bimini Bon-Boulash emerged as the winner of the mini-challenge, granting her the privilege of selecting her role for the main challenge. The main challenge required the queens to co-host a new daytime television show called Morning Glory.

On the main stage, the queens showcased their Monster Mashup runway looks. Ellie Diamond, Tayce, and Tia Kofi received positive feedback and were declared safe. The judges praised A'Whora, Bimini Bon-Boulash, and Lawrence Chaney for their performances, ultimately awarding Lawrence Chaney the challenge win. However, Ginny Lemon, Sister Sister, and Veronica Green received negative critiques.

Ginny Lemon and Sister Sister found themselves in the bottom two and had to lip-sync for their lives to the song "You Keep Me Hangin' On" by Kim Wilde. However, Ginny Lemon abruptly left the stage as soon as the song began and decided to quit the competition. It is important to note that this episode was filmed prior to the lockdown, and filming resumed later in the year.

**Departure Message:** "Witches unite! Fancy a slice?"

# QUEEN PROFILE: GINNY LEMON

Lewis Mandall, professionally known as Ginny Lemon, is a drag performer and recording artist who is celebrated for their unique and campy style of drag. Ginny attended the University of Worcester, but experienced discrimination for being gay while studying there, which ultimately led to their departure. Ginny Lemon has made appearances at Birmingham's SHOUT Festival of Queer Arts and Culture, showcasing their talent. They also had a notable appearance on The X Factor in 2017.

During their time on RuPaul's Drag Race UK, Ginny Lemon chose to eliminate themselves during a lip-sync round with fellow contestant Sister Sister. They expressed discomfort with some of the judges' comments, stating that RuPaul and Michelle Visage did not fully grasp British humour and pushed Ginny towards a more feminine-focused concept of glamour. Ginny Lemon also criticised RuPaul's emotional outburst on the show, which occurred after their departure, regarding Joe Black's outfit. They expressed their dissatisfaction on social media, highlighting the challenges faced by struggling queens who may be unable to afford elaborate costumes after months of unemployment.

In February 2022, Ginny Lemon embarked on RuPaul's Drag Race UK: The Official Tour, joining the entire cast of the show's second series for a touring event organised by World of Wonder and promoter Voss Events.

In January 2022, Ginny Lemon and fellow cast member Sister Sister appeared on the seventh series of E4's Celebrity Coach Trip, where they joined other celebrity travellers in Portugal, including Matt Richardson, Honey G, Paul Danan, The Honeyz, and Birds of a Feather stars Linda Robson and Lesley Joseph.

In July 2022, Ginny Lemon performed at the opening ceremony of the 2022 Commonwealth Games, delivering a musical act while inside a large lemon-shaped hot air balloon, dressed in a steampunk/pirate-inspired outfit.

On a personal note, Ginny identifies as non-binary. Their conversation with fellow non-binary Drag Race contestant Bimini Bon-Boulash was recognised as a catalyst in helping other non-binary individuals embrace and express their identities.

## GUEST JUDGE PROFILE: LORRAINE KELLY

Lorraine Kelly CBE, born 30th of November 1959, is a Scottish television presenter and journalist, boosting a prolific career hosting various television shows on ITV, including Good Morning Britain, GMTV, This Morning, Daybreak, The Sun Military Awards, STV Children's Appeal and her self-titled program, Lorraine.

Kelly's contributions to charity and broadcasting earned her recognition and honours. She was appointed Officer of the Order of the British Empire (OBE) in the 2012 New Year Honours for her services to charity and later promoted to Commander of the Order of the British Empire (CBE) in the 2020 Birthday Honours for her contributions to broadcasting, journalism, and charity.

Born in Glasgow's Gorbals area, Kelly spent her early years in the city before moving to East Kilbride. She attended Claremont High School and began her career in journalism by working at the East Kilbride News, her local newspaper. In 1983, she joined BBC Scotland as a researcher and later became an on-screen reporter for TV-am, covering Scottish news.

From 1984 to 1993, Kelly worked at TV-am, initially as the Scotland Correspondent and later as a presenter for Good Morning Britain alongside Mike Morris. In 1993, she played a vital role in the launch of GMTV and co-hosted the main breakfast show with Eamonn Holmes. Kelly took a maternity leave break in 1994 and returned to GMTV to host her own show, Nine O'Clock Live, which was later renamed Lorraine Live and eventually LK Today. As part of a rebranding in 2009, the show became GMTV with Lorraine. In 2010, her program was renamed Lorraine and replaced GMTV with Lorraine after GMTV's cancellation.

In addition to her work on GMTV/Lorraine, Kelly has been involved in various other projects. She presented the ITV series

Children's Hospital in 2011 and made guest appearances on shows like Never Mind the Buzzcocks and Raa Raa the Noisy Lion. Kelly also had a brief stint in radio with her own daily program on Talk Radio.

In 2012, she took over as the presenter of Daybreak, replacing Christine Bleakley. Kelly later decided to focus on her program Lorraine, which she hosted five days a week from April 2014 onwards. During her career, she made cameo appearances in Birds of a Feather and Coronation Street.

Outside of her television work, Kelly has been involved in charity initiatives. She serves as a celebrity patron for organisations such as Worldwide Cancer Research, POhWER, Help for Heroes, and The Courtyard. She participated in the BT Red Nose Desert Trek for Comic Relief in 2011 and became an ambassador for STV Children's Appeal and Sightsavers.

Kelly is also known for her writing, contributing weekly columns to The Sun and The Sunday Post. She became the first Agony Aunt for the Royal Air Force's RAF News in 2009.

Throughout her extensive career, Lorraine Kelly has made significant contributions to television presenting, journalism, and charitable events, solidifying her status as a prominent figure in the industry.

## EPISODE FIVE: "THE RURUVISION SONG CONTEST"

Following a seven-month hiatus due to lockdown, the queens made their return to the competition, with one exception. Veronica Green, unfortunately, had to withdraw from the show after testing positive for COVID-19. However, she received an open invitation to join for series 3. Meanwhile, the previously eliminated queens, except for Ginny Lemon, had the chance to compete again for a spot in the competition. After presenting their cases to the remaining contestants, Joe Black was voted by the majority to make a comeback.

For the main challenge, the contestants were tasked with writing and recording their own verses for a song to be performed in groups as part of the RuRuvision Song Contest. Lawrence Chaney and Joe Black were responsible for selecting the members of their respective groups. Lawrence Chaney, A'Whora, Bimini Bon-Boulash, and Tayce formed the group called the **United Kingdolls**. Joe Black, Ellie Diamond, Sister Sister, and Tia Kofi formed the group **Bananadrama**. The United Kingdolls emerged as the winners of the challenge, while Bananadrama received critiques during the onstage evaluations. Ellie Diamond and Sister Sister received mixed feedback but were declared safe. Joe Black and Tia Kofi faced critiques for their mainstage looks and ended up lip-syncing to "Don't Leave Me This Way" by the Communards. Ultimately, Joe Black left the competition for the second time.

**Departure Message:** "I can't be bothered writing another message. I am only capable of so many mirror messages and goodbyes. Bye. (again) See you soon!

**Queen Profile: Joe Black** (Refer to their initial elimination in episode one for their profile)

**Withdrawn: Veronica Green** (Refer to series three for their profile)

## GUEST JUDGE PROFILE: MNEK

Uzoechi Osisioma "Uzo" Emenike, known professionally as MNEK, is a talented English singer, songwriter, and record producer. Born on 9th November 1994, he has made significant contributions to the music industry and received recognition for his work. MNEK has been nominated for a Grammy and a Brit Award and has been honoured with the ASCAP Vanguard Award. His impressive list of writing and production credits includes collaborations with renowned artists such as H.E.R., Jax Jones, Zara Larsson, Little Mix, Dua Lipa, FLO, Sugababes, Clean Bandit, Julia Michaels, Craig David, Christina Aguilera, Becky Hill, Selena Gomez, Years & Years, Kylie Minogue, Beyoncé, Madonna, KSI, Mabel, and Twice.

MNEK's journey in the music industry began to unfold during his teenage years. In an interview with Build LDN, he shared his early experiences, mentioning how he started writing songs and poems at an early age. While also dabbling in music production. At 14, he uploaded some of his songs on Myspace, and one of them caught the attention of an artist named CocknBullKid (now Anita Blay), who happened to be a songwriter. This encounter led to MNEK's introduction to the music industry. Despite still being in school at the time, he had to navigate the industry while continuing his education. MNEK's collaborations with Xenomania, a production group, played a significant role in his breakthrough. His work with top acts like The Saturdays and The Wanted further solidified his position in the industry. In 2011, he released his debut single, "If Truth Be Told."

Noteworthy projects include working with AME on her debut single, "City Lights," featuring his brother Bartoven. He also contributed as a featured performer on Rudimental's songs "Spoons" and "Baby." In 2013, his contribution to the song "Need U (100%)" became one of his distinguished achievements and earned him a spot on BBC's Sound of 2014 long list.

MNEK's career continued to flourish in the following years. He collaborated with Gorgon City on the hit single "Ready for Your Love" in 2014 and worked with Madonna on her album "Rebel Heart." His debut extended play (EP) titled "Small Talk" was released in 2015, featuring the popular single "Never Forget You" with Zara Larsson. The song achieved tremendous success and received certifications in multiple countries.

Following the success of his collaborations, MNEK focused on songwriting for other artists, including Beyoncé's "Hold Up." He established partnerships with talented musicians like Becky Hill, Leo Kalyan, Shift K3Y, Ryan Ashley, Jax Jones, and Brayton Bowman. In 2018, he released his debut album, "Language," featuring the lead single "Tongue."

MNEK's influence extends beyond his music. In 2019, he organised a songwriting camp for LGBTQ+ singer-songwriters in collaboration with Pride In Music, aiming to provide a safe space for emerging talent. He has been open about his own experiences as a gay artist and hopes to support others who may be navigating their sexuality.

In 2020, MNEK achieved his first-ever vocal effort to reach number one on the Official UK Charts with the song "Head & Heart," a collaboration with Joel Corry.

## EPISODE SIX: "SNATCH GAME"

In the Snatch Game, a popular main challenge on the show, the contestants had the task of impersonating celebrities. Michelle Visage and Gemma Collins joined as contestants in this hilarious game. Here's a rundown of the cast and their chosen celebrity personas:

- A'Whora portrayed Louie Spence
- Bimini Bon-Boulash embodied Katie Price
- Ellie Diamond took on the role of Matt Lucas
- Lawrence Chaney transformed into Miriam Margolyes
- Sister Sister channelled Sally Morgan
- Tayce personified Jane Turner
- Tia Kofi depicted Mel B

After the Snatch Game, the queens showcased their runway looks, and the judges deliberated on the performances. Ellie Diamond and Sister Sister were declared safe, leaving the remaining contestants for further evaluation. Bimini Bon-Boulash emerged as the winner of the challenge, impressing the judges with their celebrity impersonation.

Tayce received positive feedback for their performance, while A'Whora received some critiques. In the end, Lawrence Chaney and Tia Kofi found themselves in the bottom two and had to lip-sync for their survival. The song they performed was "Touch Me (All Night Long)" by Cathy Dennis. Unfortunately, it was Tia Kofi who faced elimination, marking her third time in the bottom two.

**Departure Message:** "You're all camp cows! Be proud. Be kind. Give it 100% #Tiawozrobbed x"

## QUEEN PROFILE: TIA KOFI

Lawrence Bolton, professionally known as Tia Kofi, is a British drag queen hailing from Clapham, South London, born 27th of September 1990.

Tia Kofi's journey in drag began in 2014, coinciding with fellow contestant Sum Ting Wong, as they both debuted on the same day at the same venue. Their stage name is a playful take on the phrase "tea or coffee? " and during their entrance confessional on the show, Tia Kofi humorously shared that they named themselves after Tia Mowry from the sitcom "Sister Sister" and former United Nations Secretary-General Kofi Annan. Prior to their Drag Race stint, Tia Kofi regularly performed in various venues across South London, with a focus on Clapham.

Additionally, Tia Kofi is a member of the drag girl-group called The Vixens, which includes Pixie Polite and Woe Addams.

In December 2020, Tia Kofi was announced as one of the twelve contestants competing in the second series of RuPaul's Drag Race UK. Throughout the competition, Tia Kofi found herself in the bottom two lip-syncing for survival on three occasions, ultimately finishing in seventh place overall.

Shortly after their elimination from Drag Race in February 2021, Tia Kofi released their debut single, "Outside In," co-written by Little Boots, Tom Aspaul, and Gil Lewis. The accompanying music video was released on 24th of February 2021. In May 2021, Tia Kofi performed alongside series one winner The Vivienne and fellow series two contestant Veronica Green in "Drag Queens of Pop" at the Vaudeville Theatre. This performance marked one of the first shows on the West End following the third national COVID-19 lockdown in England.

In February 2022, Tia Kofi embarked on RuPaul's Drag Race UK: The Official Tour, joining the entire cast of series two in partnership with World of Wonder and promoter Voss Events. Their set included performances of "Outside In," followed by "Don't Start Now" by Dua Lipa and "No Way" from the musical Six.

Tia Kofi identifies as queer and serves as the drag mother of Victoria Scone. They use they/she pronouns.

## GUEST JUDGE PROFILE: JESSIE WARE

Jessica Lois Ware, born 15th of October 1984, is an English singer, songwriter, and broadcaster. She gained recognition with the release of her debut album, "Devotion" (2012), which reached number five on the UK Albums Chart and featured the hit single "Wildest Moments." The album was also shortlisted for the Mercury Prize. Her subsequent albums, "Tough Love" (2014) and "Glasshouse" (2017), achieved success in the UK, with the latter reaching number seven on the charts.

In 2020, Ware released her critically acclaimed fourth studio album, "What's Your Pleasure?" It peaked at number three in the UK and produced several popular singles, including "Spotlight," "Save a Kiss," and "Remember Where You Are." Her most recent album, "That! Feels Good!" (2023), reached number three in the UK and number sixteen on the Top Album Sales chart in the US. The album's lead single, "Free Yourself," was well-received by audiences.

Ware has been nominated for six Brit Awards, including Best New Artist and British Female Solo Artist. She has also ventured into other creative sectors, such as hosting the podcast "Table Manners" with her mother and launching a premium kidswear collaboration called "Anyware Kids."

In addition to her music career, Ware has been announced as one of the judges for the ITV talent show "Mamma Mia! I Have a Dream." Alongside Alan Carr, Samantha Barks, and Amber Riley, she will participate in the search for emerging musical theatre performers for the roles of Sophie and Sky in the West End production of "Mamma Mia!" as part of its 25th anniversary year.

## EPISODE SEVEN: "LOCKDOWN SUPERSHEROES"

In the reading mini challenge of the week, Sister Sister emerges as the winner, earning a 15-second head start in selecting unconventional fabrics for the "Lockdown Supersheroes" outfit. During the runway presentation, Ellie Diamond and Lawrence Chaney receive praise for their creations, while A'Whora is ultimately declared the challenge winner. However, Sister Sister and Tayce find themselves in the bottom two. Following a lip sync performance to Jess Glynne's "Don't Be So Hard on Yourself," Tayce impresses the judges and secures the victory, while Sister Sister is unfortunately eliminated from the competition.

**Departure Message:** "HATE YOUR HAIR HOPE YOU LOSE. ABSOLUTELY LOVE YOU CAMP COWS Sister Sister x"

## QUEEN PROFILE: SISTER SISTER

Philip Doran, professionally known as Sister Sister, is a renowned British drag queen hailing from Liverpool, England.

Sister Sister embarked on their drag career in 2012, drawing inspiration from notable British comedians like Dawn French, Jennifer Saunders, Victoria Wood, and drag queen Lily Savage. Their journey began in London, and in December 2020, Sister Sister was selected as one of the twelve contestants for the second season of RuPaul's Drag Race UK. During the competition, Sister Sister achieved a sixth-place finish. In February 2022, Sister Sister joined the RuPaul's Drag Race UK: The Official Tour alongside the cast of the show's second season in collaboration with World of Wonder and promoter Voss Events. Additionally, in May 2023, Sister Sister made an appearance in the trailer for the BBC coverage of the Eurovision Song Contest, which took place in Liverpool that year.

Sister Sister bravely spoke out against the online abuse they faced while participating in RuPaul's Drag Race UK's second season. In a February 2021 essay for The Guardian, the Liverpool-based entertainer revealed the distressing experience, including receiving graphic death threats from anonymous profiles. Sister Sister opened up about the severe impact this online abuse had on their mental health, stating that it reached a low point during the peak of the attacks. Discussing the matter on BBC Radio 5 Live in March 2021, Sister Sister called for more empathy and consideration in online interactions, particularly given the context of the COVID-19 pandemic. They emphasised the importance of carefully choosing words and considering the impact they may have on others, highlighting the significance of kindness in the digital age.

## GUEST JUDGE PROFILE: MAYA JAMA

Maya Indea Jama was born on 14th August 1994 in Bristol, where she attended Cotham School. She has Somali heritage from her father's side and Swedish ancestry from her mother's side. Her mother, Sadie, named her after the renowned US author and poet Maya Angelou. Jama has a close relationship with her mother and occasionally appears with her on talk shows and attends private celebrity events.

Maya Jama began her media career in London in 2012, initially aspiring to be an actress but later finding her calling as a TV presenter and fashion model. She looked up to Davina McCall and June Sarpong as her role models. Jama's early presenting gigs included hosting the weekly music video countdown on JumpOff.TV and working for Sky UK on TRACE Sports.

In 2014, she hosted "Maya's FIFA World Cup Cities" for Copa90, a travelogue covering the 2014 FIFA World Cup in Brazil. She also co-hosted the Copa90 nine-part series "World Cup Taxi" dedicated to the event. Jama joined MTV as a presenter for "The Wrap Up" in August 2014.

Throughout her career, Jama has been involved in various TV projects. She hosted the 2017 Pre-Brit Awards Party for the Brit Awards and presented a Facebook live stream from the red carpet. In 2017, she co-presented the Saturday night game show "Cannonball" on ITV. Jama also appeared as a guest panellist on ITV's "Loose Women" and co-hosted the MOBO Awards in 2017, becoming the youngest person to do so at the time.

In 2018, Jama co-presented the first series of Channel 4's "The Circle" with Alice Levine. She also co-presented "Stand Up to Cancer" with Alan Carr and Adam Hills and became the team captain on ITV2's rap panel show "Don't Hate the Playaz." In 2019, she appeared on "A League of Their Own Road Trip" and featured on Channel 4's "The Big Fat Quiz of the Year" in 2019 and 2020.

Maya Jama presented the BBC One TV programme "Peter Crouch: Save Our Summer" in 2020 and co-presented BBC One's New Year's Eve programme "The Big New Year's In." In 2021, she took over as the presenter of "Glow Up: Britain's Next Make-Up Star". In 2021, it was announced that Jama would be the host of Simon Cowell's music competition gameshow "Walk The Line." And in 2022, she was announced as the new presenter of ITV2's "Love Island," succeeding Laura Whitmore.

From 2014 to 2017, Maya Jama hosted #DriveWithMaya, a weekday show on Rinse FM. In 2018, she joined BBC Radio 1, co-presenting Radio 1's Greatest Hits on Saturdays and hosting her own show, "Maya Jama," on Fridays and Saturdays. However, in May 2020, she announced her departure from Radio 1, citing exciting new commitments that prevented her from continuing her contract.

## EPISODE EIGHT: "STONED ON THE RUNWAY"

During the mini challenge, the queens are tasked with delivering a "butch" rendition of RuPaul's single "Kitty Girl." Ellie Diamond impresses the judges and emerges as the winner, granting her the power to determine the order for the stand-up comedy challenge. This decision sparks resentment among the other queens.

On the runway, the judges express their criticism towards A'Whora's comedy routine, deeming it overly sexual. Conversely, Bimini receives accolades for their comedic performance and innovative interpretation of the runway theme. As a result, A'Whora and Tayce find themselves in the bottom two, requiring them to lip-sync for their lives. They showcase their talents to Dusty Springfield's "You Don't Have to Say You Love Me," but it is A'Whora who ultimately faces elimination from the competition.

**Departure Message:** "Talk about Sexual TENSION!! I'll See you all at the Sauna Lots of love A'Whora xoxo"

## QUEEN PROFILE: A'WHORA

George Boyle, professionally known as A'Whora, is a British drag queen hailing from Worksop, England. Boyle's journey in the fashion industry began at the age of 16 when he pursued a diploma in womenswear and fashion at a college in Mansfield. He successfully graduated in 2013. Subsequently, he moved to London in 2015 to further his studies at the London College of Fashion, where he obtained a bachelor's degree in womenswear in 2018.

Boyle has also made a name for himself as a model; notable highlights of his professional journey include creating a sustainable 10-piece collection for H&M in 2015, working with esteemed brands such as Kurt Geiger and John Lewis & Partners, and gracing the pages of Vogue Italia. Additionally, he has founded his own fashion label called Le'Boy George.

In December 2020, A'Whora gained recognition as one of the twelve contestants on the second series of RuPaul's Drag Race UK, ultimately finishing in fifth place. He embarked on a successful UK Tour, the United Kingdolls Tour, alongside Tayce, Bimini Bon Boulash, and Lawrence Chaney in July 2021, organised by Klub Kids. A'Whora also had the opportunity to walk the runway at London Fashion Week in February 2021, representing the London-based fashion brand Art School alongside fellow contestant Bimini Bon-Boulash, with designs by Eden Loweth.

At the time of filming, A'Whora resided in Streatham, South London, sharing a living space with fellow RuPaul's Drag Race UK contestant Tayce.

## GUEST JUDGE PROFILE: DAWN FRENCH

Dawn Roma French, born on the 11th of October 1957, is a British actress, comedian, presenter, and writer. She is best known for her work on the BBC comedy sketch show "French and Saunders," which she co-wrote and starred in with her comedy partner Jennifer Saunders. French also played the lead role of Geraldine Granger in the BBC sitcom "The Vicar of Dibley." Throughout her career, she has been nominated for seven BAFTA TV Awards and received a BAFTA Fellowship in 2009.

French was born in Holyhead, Wales, to English parents Felicity Roma and Denys Vernon French. Her father served in the Royal Air Force, and her family moved frequently due to his postings. French attended various schools, including Caistor Grammar School and St Dunstan's Abbey School for Girls in Plymouth. She later studied at the Spence School in New York on a debating scholarship.

While studying drama at the Royal Central School of Speech and Drama in 1977, French met Jennifer Saunders, her future comedy partner. Initially, they did not get along, as French aspired to be a drama teacher while Saunders had no interest in that career path. However, they eventually became friends and decided to form a comedy double-act called the Menopause Sisters. Their comedic talents gained attention as members of the Comic Strip, an alternative comedy group in the early 1980s.

French's television career took off when she appeared in Channel 4's "The Comic Strip Presents" series in 1982. She acted in numerous episodes and wrote two of them. French and Saunders went on to create their own comedy series, "French & Saunders," which debuted in 1987. The duo gained recognition for their celebrity parodies and film spoofs. French also had successful solo ventures, such as her role in "The Vicar of Dibley," which became one of her most iconic roles.

Apart from television, French has also acted in films, including "The Adventures of Pinocchio," "Harry Potter and the Prisoner of Azkaban," and "The Chronicles of Narnia: The Lion, the Witch and the Wardrobe." She has appeared in theatre productions such as "A Midsummer Night's Dream" and "My Brilliant Divorce."

In addition to her acting career, French is an accomplished writer. She has written an autobiography titled "Dear Fatty," which consists of letters to important people in her life. She has also penned novels, including "A Tiny Bit Marvellous" and "According to Yes."

French's talent and contributions to the entertainment industry have earned her widespread acclaim. She continues to be a beloved figure in British comedy and entertainment, with her work spanning television, film, theatre, writing, and even music videos.

# EPISODE NINE: "BEASTENDERS"

In this week's mini-challenge, the queens are given the delightful task of creating adorned puppets to impersonate their fellow queens. Bimini Bon-Boulash rises to the occasion and emerges as the victor, earning the privilege to assign roles for the captivating BeastEnders acting challenge. Bimini opts to portray Scat Slater, while Tayce embodies the essence of Karen Bitchell. Ellie Diamond skilfully takes on the character of Thot Bottom, and Lawrence Chaney brilliantly embodies Phyllis Bitchell.

Each queen receives praise for their performances, but it is Bimini who ultimately claims the crown for this challenge. Lawrence finds safety in their performance, leaving Ellie Diamond and Tayce to engage in a thrilling lip sync battle to the beats of "Last Thing on My Mind" by Steps. In a surprising twist, RuPaul decides it is a tie, declaring a double shantay and granting both Tayce and Ellie Diamond the opportunity to advance to the highly anticipated finale.

## QUEEN PROFILE: ELLIE DIAMOND

Elliot Glen, born 20th of December 1998, is a talented Scottish drag performer who is widely known by the stage name Ellie Diamond.

Ellie Diamond embarked on her journey as a drag performer in Dundee back in 2015. Despite the absence of an established drag scene in the area, she aspires to ignite its creation and foster its growth. Her drag name is a clever fusion of her birth name, Elliot, with inspiration drawn from notable British singers such as Ellie Goulding, Marina and The Diamonds, and Hannah Diamond. When in drag, Ellie radiates like a dazzling diamond, hence her chosen moniker.

In December 2020, Ellie Diamond's talent was recognised as she was selected as one of the twelve contestants for the second series of RuPaul's Drag Race UK. Throughout the competition, she showcased her skills and unique flair, ultimately securing a commendable fourth place overall. In March 2021, Ellie, alongside her fellow RuPaul's Drag Race UK finalists Lawrence Chaney, Bimini Bon Boulash, and Tayce, had the opportunity to be featured in a photoshoot and interview for The Guardian and later graced the pages of British Vogue.

Exciting prospects awaited Ellie Diamond as she embarked on the RuPaul's Drag Race UK: The Official Tour in February 2022. This tour offered an incredible platform for Ellie to showcase her artistry to an even broader audience and connect with fans across the country.

# EPISODE TEN: "GRAND FINALE"
# RUNNER-UP: TAYCE

Tayce Szura-Radix, born on 28th May 1994, is a remarkable drag queen, rapper, and model hailing from Newport, Wales.

Tayce embarked on her professional career as a drag queen in 2017, starting off her journey at Revolution Newport, a popular vodka bar. When in drag, Tayce draws inspiration from iconic performers like Beyoncé, Ciara, and Jennifer Lopez, allowing their artistry to influence her own unique style. In January 2020, she had the honour of attending the inaugural RuPaul's DragCon UK, where she took the main stage and performed alongside acclaimed queens Shea Couleé and Ore-Ho.

In December 2020, Tayce's talent and charisma earned her a spot among the twelve contestants competing in the second series of RuPaul's Drag Race UK. Throughout the competition, Tayce showcased her skills and emerged victorious in Episode 5's main challenge, "The RuRuvision Song Contest," alongside A'Whora, Bimini Bon-Boulash, and Lawrence Chaney, earning herself a prestigious RuPeter badge. While she found herself in the bottom two on four occasions, Tayce's lip-sync performances were nothing short of sensational. She won three lip-sync battles, eliminating Cherry Valentine, Sister Sister, and A'Whora in the process. Her fourth lip-sync against Ellie Diamond resulted in a "double-shantay," where both queens advanced to the finale, making Tayce the first queen in RuPaul's Drag Race UK series history to survive four lip-syncs and win three of them. Fans affectionately dubbed her a "lip-sync assassin."

Tayce's captivating performances are frequently showcased at nightclubs, with London being a primary location for her shows.

In May 2021, she captivated audiences as a featured performer at Drive Time Drag, a pioneering drag drive-in show in the United Kingdom. In July 2021, Tayce embarked on a highly successful sold-out UK Tour alongside A'Whora, Bimini Bon-Boulash, and Lawrence Chaney, known as the United Kingdolls Tour, presented by promoter Klub Kids.

In March 2021, Tayce proudly announced her role as an ambassador for Coca-Cola's "Open That Cola!" campaign in the United Kingdom. As of June 2021, she ranks as the second most followed drag queen within the Drag Race UK franchise on Instagram.

Tayce's captivating presence and talent have attracted significant attention in the media. In April 2021, she was interviewed for and featured on the cover of Attitude's "Tea Time digital special." Later that month, Tayce, alongside fellow Drag Race contestant A'Whora, co-launched The Bluebella Pride, a lingerie line advocating for the abolition of anti-gay laws in 35 Commonwealth nations. In June 2021, Tayce partnered with Nasty Gal, a fashion brand owned by Boohoo, for an exciting 60-piece gender-neutral capsule collection.

As a model, Tayce currently holds a contract with Models 1 modelling agency, representing both her in-drag and out-of-drag personas. She has graced the runways of London and Paris Fashion Weeks and has been featured in two Jean Paul Gaultier fragrance campaigns.

Tayce is the son of Roger Radix, a former bass guitarist for Wham! She currently resides in Streatham, South London, England, and previously lived with fellow RuPaul's Drag Race UK contestant A'Whora. In a poignant moment on episode eight of RuPaul's Drag Race UK, Tayce bravely shared her experience of being diagnosed with chlamydia and gonorrhoea at the age of 18, which significantly impacted her self-esteem and altered her perspective on relationships due to feelings of shame and guilt. Her openness in discussing this experience was widely praised for breaking down stigmas surrounding sexually transmitted infections, including a commendation from the British charity the Terrence Higgins Trust. Tayce identifies as gay and uses she/her pronouns while in drag and he/him pronouns when out of drag.

## RUNNER-UP: BIMINI BON-BOULASH

Bimini Bon-Boulash, known simply as Bimini, was born as Thomas Hibbitts on 12th of May 1993 in Great Yarmouth, England. They are an English drag queen, author, recording artist, and model based in East London.

Bimini attended Lynn Grove Academy and later moved to London in 2012 to study journalism at the London College of Communication. It was in London that Bimini discovered drag and began their journey as a drag performer in 2017. Since 2019, Bimini has been dedicated to their career as a drag queen. Their unique style and aesthetic draw inspiration from fashion icons such as Alexander McQueen, Vivienne Westwood, Iris van Herpen, and John Galliano. Bimini's look is heavily influenced by Pamela Anderson, and their drag name combines what they might have been called if assigned female at birth and the name of their first cat, Bonnie Boulash.

Based in East London, Bimini frequently performs in various venues across the capital city.

During their time on the second series of RuPaul's Drag Race UK, they showcased their talent from the start, winning a lip-sync battle against Joe Black to "Relax" by Frankie Goes to Hollywood in the first episode. Bimini went on to win four challenges, including the Snatch Game, where they portrayed Katie Price, making them the first contestant in the British version of the show to achieve this act. In Episode nine, Bimini became the first contestant to secure a spot in the finale after lip-syncing in the first episode. In the final episode, after an intense lip-sync battle, they were announced as a runner-up alongside Tayce.

In February 2021, Bimini made their runway debut at London Fashion Week for Art School London, a genderless fashion label, alongside fellow Drag Race contestant A'Whora. They were featured in a photoshoot and interview for The Guardian in March 2021, along with the other Drag Race UK finalists. In July 2021, Bimini embarked on a successful sold-out UK tour called the United Kingdolls Tour alongside A'Whora, Tayce, and Lawrence Chaney, presented by Klub Kids.

In March 2021, Bimini announced through their Instagram account that they would be writing a book titled "A Drag Queen's Guide to Life," which was later released in October 2021 with the title "Release the Beast: A Drag Queen's Guide to Life." Published by Penguin Books and Viking Books, the book covers various aspects of life and incorporates their verse from "UK Hun?", performed with The United Kingdolls.

Bimini also ventured into the music industry, releasing their debut single, "God Save This Queen" in June 2021, accompanied by a music video. In August 2021, Bimini co-hosted the Saturday afternoon slot on BBC Radio 1 as part of the station's "drag day," alongside Dean McCullough. They also made a cameo appearance in the 2021 Christmas advertisement for Sainsbury's, a well-known supermarket chain in the UK.

In November 2021, Bimini received the Drag Hero award at the GAY TIMES Honours ceremony in London, where they were also featured as the cover star for the GAY TIMES Honours edition.

Bimini identifies as non-binary, using they/them pronouns when out of drag and she/her pronouns when in drag. They openly discussed their gender identity in a heartfelt conversation with fellow non-binary contestant Ginny Lemon on Drag Race. Their openness and honesty were commended by viewers and encouraged others to have similar conversations about gender identity with their loved ones. Bimini has been following an exclusively vegan diet for eight years.

## SERIES TWO WINNER: LAWRENCE CHANEY

Lawrence Chaney, born Lawrence Maidment on 16th of October 1996, is a drag queen based in Glasgow, Scotland. They gained fame by winning the second series of RuPaul's Drag Race UK, making history as the first Scottish drag queen to win in the franchise. This achievement also earned them the 2021 BAFTA Scotland Audience Award. As a result of their success on the show, Chaney was granted their own online television series called Tartan Around, which premiered in 2022.

Chaney began their professional drag career in Glasgow in 2014. In an interview with Metro, they explained that their drag surname "Chaney" was inspired by Lon Chaney, a renowned silent movie star from the 1920s known as the "man of a thousand faces." They compared themselves to the "queen of a thousand faces" due to their skill in impersonation, silly voices, and general buffoonery.

Following their Drag Race success, Chaney was featured in The Guardian and British Vogue alongside their fellow finalists. They also embarked on the United Kingdolls Tour and participated in RuPaul's Drag Race UK: The Official Tour.

Chaney has been featured on the cover of Attitude's "Tea Time Digital Special" and was interviewed for various publications.

They were also a guest at the digital National Student Pride 2021 event. In May 2021, it was announced that Transworld had acquired the rights to publish Chaney's memoir, Lawrence (Drag) Queen of Scots: The Dos and Don'ts of a Drag Superstar.

Before RuPaul's Drag Race UK, Chaney collaborated frequently with the BBC, particularly BBC Sounds. They even hosted a Saturday mid-morning slot on BBC Radio 1 as part of "Drag Day" in August 2021, alongside Arielle Free and other drag queens.

Chaney grew up in Helensburgh, Scotland, and Newbury, England. They currently reside in the Gorbals area of Glasgow and have expressed support for Scottish independence. Chaney has publicly discussed their struggles with gender identity, describing themselves as fluid and constantly evolving. They prefer the use of they/them pronouns.

| Contestant | Age | Hometown | Result |
|---|---|---|---|
| Lawrence Chaney | 23 | Glasgow, Scotland | Winner |
| Bimini Bon-Boulash | 26 | Great Yarmouth, England | Runner-up |
| Tayce | 25 | Newport, Wales | Runner-up |
| Ellie Diamond | 21 | Dundee, Scotland | 4th place |
| A'Whora | 23 | Worksop, England | 5th place |
| Sister Sister | 31 | Liverpool, England | 6th place |
| Tia Kofi | 30 | South London, England | 7th place |
| Joe Black | 30 | Brighton, England | 8th place |
| Veronica Green | 34 | Rochdale, England | 9th place |
| Ginny Lemon | 31 | Worcester, England | 10th place |
| Asttina Mandella | 27 | East London, England | 11th place |
| Cherry Valentine | 26 | Darlington, England | 12th place |

*Information correct at time of filming*

# RUPAUL'S DRAG RACE UK SERIES 3

The third series of RuPaul's Drag Race UK commenced its broadcast on 23rd of September 2021

On the 18th of August 2021, the official cast of the third series was announced through social media platforms. Notably, Veronica Green made a comeback after having to withdraw from the second series due to a positive COVID-19 test. She received an open invitation to participate in the third series. Additionally, Victoria Scone joined as the franchise's first-ever cisgender female contestant since its inception in 2009.

## EPISODE ONE: "THE RETURN OF ROYALTY"

In the werkroom, 11 new queens representing different regions of the UK made their entrance. Notably, Veronica Green returned to the competition after her withdrawal from the previous series due to COVID-19. The queens were tasked with a mini challenge that required them to pair up and play "Ru's Dirty Charade." For the main challenge, each queen had to showcase two runway looks: "Queen of Your Home Town" and "My Favourite Things."

During the runway presentation, Krystal Versace, Scarlett Harlett, and Victoria Scone received high praise for their captivating looks. However, Anubis, Elektra Fence, and River Medway faced negative critiques for their runway presentations. The judges announced Krystal Versace and Victoria Scone as the top two queens of the week, who would battle it out in a lip-sync to Bonnie Tyler's "Total Eclipse of the Heart" for the chance to win the challenge. Ultimately, Krystal Versace emerged as the victorious queen. River Medway was declared safe, while Anubis and Elektra Fence found themselves as the bottom two queens. They engaged in a lip-sync showdown to the tune of "Sweet Melody" by Little Mix. Elektra Fence triumphed in the lip-sync, leading to Anubis sashaying away from the competition.

**Departure Message:** Camp as tits darling! The Curse of Brighton lives on... Love you all! Anubis

## QUEEN PROFILE: ANUBIS

Charli Paul Frank Monét Finch, professionally known as Anubis Finch or simply Anubis, is an English drag queen and singer. Born on 14th of August 2001, in Seaford, East Sussex, Charli Finch experienced a significant loss when their father passed away when they were 16 years old. Motivated by this event, they underwent a remarkable physical transformation, losing nine stone, and embarked on their journey as a drag queen under the name Anubis Finch. The name Anubis was chosen as a tribute to their father's Egyptian heritage.

In 2019, Anubis released their debut extended play, Anubis, showcasing their musical artistry. They later followed up with a cover of "Have Yourself A Merry Little Christmas" the same year. Their musical journey continued in 2020 with the release of another single titled "Home."

In 2021, Anubis was announced as one of the contestants competing in the highly anticipated third series of RuPaul's Drag Race UK. Unfortunately, they were the first contestant to be eliminated from the competition after losing a lip sync against Elektra Fence. Despite this setback, Anubis was later bestowed with the title of Miss Congeniality by their fellow competitors, highlighting their positive and supportive presence.

In 2022, Finch released their single "Wonderland" and embarked on the RuPaul's Drag Race UK: The Official Tour, joining the cast of the third series in entertaining audiences across the country.

## GUEST JUDGE PROFILE: MATT LUCAS

Matthew Richard Lucas is a versatile English actor, comedian, writer, and television presenter. He gained widespread recognition for his collaboration with David Walliams on the popular BBC sketch comedy series Little Britain (2003-2006), and Come Fly with Me (2010-2011). Lucas initially rose to fame as the scorekeeper George Dawes on the comedy panel show Shooting Stars from 1995 to 2009. He also portrayed the character Nardole in the BBC series Doctor Who from 2015 to 2017. In addition to his television work, Lucas has appeared in several films, including Astro Boy (2009), Alice in Wonderland (2010), Bridesmaids (2011), Gnomeo & Juliet (2011), Small Apartments (2012), and Paddington (2014). From 2020 to 2023, Lucas co-hosted The Great British Bake Off alongside Noel Fielding.

Matthew Richard Lucas was born on 5th of March 1974, in the Paddington area of London. His parents, Diana and John Stanley Lucas, owned a chauffeuring business. Lucas comes from a Jewish background, with his mother's family having fled Nazi Germany before World War II. He grew up in a Reform Jewish household, although his parents came from Orthodox Jewish families. At a young age, Lucas developed alopecia, which resulted in him losing all his hair by the age of six in 1980.

Lucas attended Aylward Primary School and later Haberdashers' Boys' School in Borehamwood, Hertfordshire. During his time at the University of Bristol from 1992 to 1995, where he studied drama, Lucas crossed paths with his future collaborator, David

Walliams. He also spent time with the National Youth Theatre during this period.

Lucas's career took off when he joined forces with Vic Reeves and Bob Mortimer in 1992. He appeared in The Smell of Reeves and Mortimer in 1995 and became well-known for his portrayal of George Dawes on Shooting Stars. Lucas continued his collaboration with Reeves and Mortimer in shows like Randall & Hopkirk (Deceased) and Catterick, playing various roles. In 1999, he partnered with David Walliams to create Rock Profile, a comedy show parodying famous musicians.

Lucas gained significant success with Little Britain, a radio show that later became a television series. Alongside Walliams, Lucas showcased his talent by portraying various iconic characters, including Andy Pipkin, Vicky Pollard, Daffyd Thomas, and Marjorie Dawes. The duo's comedic skills were widely acclaimed, and they were hailed as the most influential figures in TV comedy by Radio Times in 2005.

Lucas diversified his career by taking on dramatic roles, such as his supporting part in the BBC historical serial Casanova (2005) and voice work in King Arthur's Disasters (2005). He also appeared in films like Alice in Wonderland (2010) and played a role in the comedy Bridesmaids (2011). Lucas expanded his repertoire by hosting his own radio show, And The Winner Is, from February 2010.

Lucas and Walliams returned to television with their series Come Fly with Me in 2010, focusing on the airline industry. He further demonstrated his versatility by appearing in stage musicals, such as Taboo in 2002, where he portrayed Leigh Bowery.

## EPISODE TWO: "DRAGOTON"

As the queens gather in the werkroom following the first elimination, Victoria Scone reveals that she has injured her knee during the lip-sync. Meanwhile, Krystal Versace, the previous challenge winner, is given the task of conducting a peer-assessment mini-challenge. She evaluates her fellow queens in five categories:

- Star Buy (The Biggest Competition)
- Bargain Bin (The Trashiest Taste)
- Hot Deal (The Trade of the Season)
- Out of Date (The Totally Irrelevant Queen)
- BOGOF (Next Eliminated Queen)

Krystal selects Victoria Scone, River Medway, Ella Vaday, Veronica Green, and Elektra Fence for each respective category.

Moving on to the week's main challenge, the queens are divided into teams and tasked with portraying dance instructors for the brand-new fitness concept called Dragoton. Team Ride or Die consists of Choriza May, Elektra Fence, and Vanity Milan. Team Ball Busters comprises Kitty Scott-Claus, Krystal Versace, River Medway, and Veronica Green. Lastly, Team Babycizers includes Charity Kase, Ella Vaday, Scarlett Harlett, and Victoria Scone.

On the main stage, the queens showcase their Red-Carpet Showstoppers. Kitty Scott-Claus, Krystal Versace, and Veronica Green receive positive critiques, with Krystal Versace ultimately winning the challenge. However, Charity Kase, Elektra Fence, and Vanity Milan face negative critiques, and Charity Kase is declared safe. This leads to a lip-sync battle between Elektra Fence and Vanity Milan, performing to "Moving On Up" by M People. Vanity Milan emerges victorious in the lip-sync, while Elektra Fence sashays away. Following the lip-sync, Victoria Scone is called to the front of the stage to seek medical advice regarding her injured knee.

**Departure Message:** I couldn't reach. Only joking.. Love Vanity

## QUEEN PROFILE: ELEKTRA FENCE

Julian Riley, professionally known as Elektra Fence was born in Burnley, Lancashire, Julian grew up in a family where both parents had cerebral palsy. Tragically, one of her brothers passed away during her teenage years. It was during this time that she began exploring drag performance and adopted the stage name Elektra Fence. The name was inspired by a viral video of Julian playfully touching an electric fence, capturing the attention of social media audiences.

In 2021, Elektra Fence was announced as one of the contestants competing on the third series of RuPaul's Drag Race UK, showcasing her talent on a larger platform. In the first episode, she faced off against Anubis Finch in a lip sync battle to "Sweet Melody" by Little Mix and emerged victorious, securing her spot in the competition. However, the following week, Elektra found herself in the bottom two once again, this time lip syncing against Vanity Milan to "Moving on Up" by M People. Unfortunately, she was eliminated from the competition at that point.

Outside of the show, Elektra Fence experienced a distressing incident in 2022 when she became the target of a homophobic assault while on a train. This unfortunate event shed light on the ongoing challenges faced by the LGBTQ+ community.

## GUEST JUDGE PROFILE: OTI MABUSE

Otlile "Oti" Mabuse, born 8th August 1990, is a South African talent show judge, presenter, dancer, and Latin dance champion. Currently based in the United Kingdom, she is widely recognised for her role as a professional dancer on the British television series Strictly Come Dancing, which she won in both 2019 and 2020. She has also made a name for herself on Let's Dance, the German equivalent of Strictly Come Dancing, and has served as a Dance Captain on The Greatest Dancer. In addition, Oti has been a panellist on The Masked Dancer since 2021 and became a judge on Dancing on Ice in 2022.

Oti Mabuse was born in Pretoria and initially pursued civil engineering at university before embarking on a career in professional ballroom dancing. Her elder sister, Motsi Mabuse, is also a professional ballroom dancer. Oti's dancing journey has been remarkable, having won the South African Latin American Championship a staggering eight times. Seeking new opportunities and growth, she eventually moved to Germany. Throughout her dancing career, Oti has earned several notable titles, including third place in the World Cup Freestyle Latin in 2014, second place in the European Championship Latin in 2014, and first place in the German Championship PD Freestyle Latin.

In 2015, Oti Mabuse made her debut as a professional dancer on the eighth season of Let's Dance, showcasing her talent and expertise to a wider audience. She was paired with singer Daniel Küblböck, and together they impressed viewers. Unfortunately, the couple was eliminated in week 9, finishing in sixth place.

Returning for the ninth season of Let's Dance in 2016, Oti continued to shine as a professional dancer. This time, she was partnered with television presenter Niels Ruf. However, their journey on the show was short-lived as they were the first couple to be eliminated, leaving the competition in 14th place.

## EPISODE THREE: "GREAT OUTDOORS"

RuPaul announces to the remaining contestants that Victoria Scone had withdrawn from the competition due to her knee injury. The mini challenge for the week involves creating profile videos for the new dating app Findhr. Scarlett Harlett impresses the judges and emerges as the winner of the mini challenge.

For the main challenge, the queens are tasked with designing two outfits using camping materials: Happy Campers and Campfire Couture.

On the runway, Ella Vaday, Krystal Versace, and Scarlett Harlett receive high praise for their creative looks. Ultimately, Scarlett Harlett secures the win for the main challenge. However, Choriza May lands in the safe zone after receiving mixed critiques.

Vanity Milan and Veronica Green face criticism for their outfits during the main challenge and find themselves in the bottom two. They engage in a lip-sync battle, performing to the song "I've Got the Music in Me" by The Kiki Dee Band. Vanity Milan delivers an exceptional performance and emerges as the winner of the lip-sync. As a result, Veronica Green is eliminated from the competition.

**Departure Message:** The party may be over for me here, But I'll see you all at the Afterparty! All my love Veronica Green xxx

## QUEEN PROFILE (ELIMINATED): VERONICA GREEN

Veronica Green, born Kevin Max Grogan, is a popular British drag performer who gained recognition through her appearances on the second and third series of RuPaul's Drag Race UK.

Before joining RuPaul's Drag Race, Veronica Green showcased her talent on the BBC One music reality television show All Together

Now. During her performance, she caught the attention of fellow Drag Race UK contestant Divina de Campo. Her impressive skills earned her a spot on the second series of RuPaul's Drag Race UK, which was announced in December 2020. Unfortunately, Green had to leave the competition after contracting COVID-19, placing ninth overall.

Despite her early exit, Veronica Green received an open invitation to return for the third series of RuPaul's Drag Race UK. She made it to the third week of the competition before facing elimination in a lip sync battle against Vanity Milan, once again placing ninth.

In May 2021, Green took part in the highly anticipated show Drag Queens of Pop, performing alongside The Vivienne, the winner of the first series, and Tia Kofi, another contestant from the second series. The show, held at the Vaudeville Theatre, marked one of the first performances on London's West End after the third national COVID-19 lockdown in England.

Continuing her creative pursuits, Veronica Green released a collaborative single titled "Nothing To Lose" with Myleene Klass in October 2021. She also appeared in a television and online ad campaign for Bailey's Irish Cream, alongside fellow drag queens Tia Kofi and Asia Thorne, portraying three witches. The ad campaign reached audiences not only in the UK but also in Australia and the United States.

## QUEEN PROFILE (WITHDRAWN): VICTORIA SCONE

Victoria Scone, born Emily Diapre on 6$^{th}$ of April 1993, is a British drag queen and cabaret performer hailing from Cardiff, Wales. She gained prominence as a contestant on the third series of RuPaul's Drag Race UK in 2021, where she made history as the first cisgender female competitor in the entire Drag Race franchise. In 2022, she returned to the competition scene by participating in Canada's Drag Race: Canada vs. the World.

Emily Diapre has a professional background in acting, singing, and dancing. Prior to fully embracing drag as a career, she worked as a sales and events coordinator. When selecting her stage name, she opted for Victoria Scone to evoke a distinctly British feel. The name choice reflects her curvaceous figure, and she also enjoys the playful pun of "Victoria's gone" as part of her name's wordplay.

Victoria Scone rose to prominence during her stint on the third series of RuPaul's Drag Race UK. Her participation marked a significant milestone as the first cisgender female contestant in the history of the Drag Race franchise. At the time of her appearance on the show, she had been involved in drag for approximately three years. She showcased her talent early on and even placed in the top two during the first episode. However, on the third episode, Victoria made the difficult decision to withdraw from the competition after partially tearing her anterior cruciate ligament during a top-two lip sync for the win against Krystal Versace.

Victoria Scone returned to the Drag Race stage to compete in Canada's Drag Race: Canada vs. the World, where she faced off against former contestants from various iterations of the Drag Race franchise. Among her competitors was Vanity Milan, a fellow alum from RuPaul's Drag Race UK series three. Throughout her time in the competition, Victoria achieved impressive results, landing in the top two on three occasions and never facing elimination. She reached the finale but ultimately lost in a lip-sync against the eventual season winner, Ra'Jah O'Hara, during the first round of the Lip-Sync for the Crown tournament. As a result, she tied for third place alongside fellow competitor Rita Baga.

## GUEST JUDGE PROFILE: NICOLA COUGHLAN

Nicola Mary Coughlan, born 9th January 1987, is an Irish actress known for her notable roles as Clare Devlin in the Channel 4 sitcom Derry Girls and Penelope Featherington in the Netflix period drama Bridgerton.

Coughlan was born and raised in Galway, Ireland, specifically in Oranmore. At the young age of five, while watching her older sister perform in a school play, she discovered her passion for acting. She attended Scoil Mhuire for primary school and Calasanctius College for secondary school. Later, she pursued a degree in English and Classical Civilisation at the National University of Ireland, Galway. She studied at the Oxford School of Drama and Birmingham School of Acting in England to further her training.

Coughlan's acting journey began at the age of 10 in 1997, with an uncredited role in the action thriller film My Brother's War. In 2004, she embarked on her career by appearing in Tom Collins' short film, The Phantom Cnut, a revenge comedy. Over the years, she lent her voice to various animated series. However, due to financial challenges, Coughlan had to return to Ireland, where she battled depression with the support of her family. During this time, she worked part-time at an optician in Galway. In a stroke of luck, she responded to an open casting call for Jess and Joe Forever at The Old Vic in London and landed the lead role of Jess. The play premiered in September 2016, followed by a national tour.

In 2018, Coughlan gained widespread recognition for her portrayal of Clare Devlin, one of the main characters in the sitcom Derry Girls, set in 1990s Derry, Northern Ireland. Originally broadcast on Channel 4 in January and February 2018, the show achieved international success after its release on Netflix in December of the same year.

In that same year, Coughlan also played Hannah Dalton in the period drama series Harlots, set in 18th-century London. She made her West End debut in The Prime of Miss Jean Brodie at The Donmar Warehouse, earning recognition as one of the Rising Stars of 2018 by the Evening Standard. Additionally, she competed alongside some of her Derry Girls co-stars in an episode of The Great British Bake Off.

In 2019, Coughlan's casting in the Netflix series Bridgerton was announced. The show, based on Julia Quinn's best-selling book series, premiered in December 2020. Coughlan portrays Penelope Featherington, the youngest daughter of a newly wealthy family in Regency-era London.

Coughlan has actively engaged in charity work and advocacy. In 2018, during her time performing in The Prime of Miss Jean Brodie, she wrote a piece for The Guardian addressing the unfair scrutiny of women's bodies in theatre criticism. She also made headlines for her response to the Daily Mirror's comment on her appearance at the 2019 British Academy Television Awards, confidently stating that she looked "smokin'."

In July 2020, Coughlan auctioned off an Alex Perry dress, raising €5,000 for the Laura Lynn Hospice, an Irish children's hospice providing specialised palliative and supportive care services. Furthermore, in February 2019, she joined 28 women in a symbolic march across London's Westminster Bridge, advocating for the decriminalisation of abortion in Northern Ireland. The march represented the estimated number of women who had to travel to England each week to access abortion services.

In June 2020, Coughlan and her fellow Derry Girls co-stars, along with Saoirse Ronan, performed a sketch for the RTÉ fundraising special RTÉ Does Comic Relief, with the proceeds going to those affected by the COVID-19 pandemic.

# EPISODE FOUR: "BIG DRAG ENERGY"

In this week's main challenge, the queens are divided into teams and tasked with writing and performing individual verses for the song "Big Drag Energy". The members of Team **Slice Girls** are Charity Kase, Kitty Scott-Klaus, Krystal Versace, and Scarlett Harlett. Meanwhile, Team **Pick 'n' Mix** consists of Choriza May, Ella Vaday, River Medway, and Vanity Milan.

On the runway, the theme is Night of a Thousand Spice Girls. After deliberation, Team Pick 'n' Mix emerges as the victor of the challenge, while Team Slice Girls finds themselves on the losing end. The bottom two queens of the week are revealed to be Charity Kase and Scarlett Harlett. They engage in a lip-sync battle to "Who Do You Think You Are" by Spice Girls. Both queens deliver outstanding performances, resulting in a double win for the lip-sync, allowing them to continue their journey in the competition.

## GUEST JUDGE PROFILE: EMMA BUNTON

Emma Lee Bunton, born 21$^{st}$ of January 1976, is an English singer, songwriter, actress, and media personality. She gained fame in the 1990s as a member of the girl group Spice Girls, where she was known as Baby Spice. The group sold over 100 million records worldwide, making them the best-selling female group of all time.

During the Spice Girls hiatus, Bunton released her first solo album, "A Girl Like Me" (2001), which debuted at number four on the UK Albums Chart and achieved gold certification for sales exceeding 100,000 copies. The album featured the hit single "What Took You So Long?", which topped the UK Singles Chart. Her second studio album, "Free Me" (2004), included the successful singles "Free Me," "Maybe," and "I'll Be There." Bunton's third studio album, "Life in Mono" (2006), featured the top three single "Downtown." In 2019, she released her fourth studio album, "My Happy Place." She also reunited with the Spice Girls for tours in 2007 and 2019.

Aside from her music career, Bunton has made various television appearances. She had a recurring role on the BBC One comedy series "Absolutely Fabulous" (2003-2012), participated in the fourth series of the BBC dancing competition show "Strictly Come Dancing," and served as a judge on the ITV celebrity skating show "Dancing on Ice" (2010–2011) and the entertainment series "Your Face Sounds Familiar" (2013). She was a radio presenter on the Heart Breakfast Show in London from 2013 to 2018 and currently hosts her own show on Sunday evenings.

Bunton was born in Finchley, Barnet, London. She attended St Theresa's Roman Catholic Primary School and later enrolled in the Sylvia Young Theatre School. She appeared in several TV shows, including the BBC soap opera "EastEnders" and the ITV police drama "The Bill." Bunton's music career took off when she joined the Spice Girls in 1994, and they went on to achieve massive success with hits like "Wannabe," "Say You'll Be There," and "Spice Up Your Life."

In recent years, Bunton has been involved in projects such as the Spice Girls musical "Viva Forever" and performed with the group at the 2012 Summer Olympics closing ceremony. She released her solo album "My Happy Place" in 2019 and continues to pursue various entertainment ventures.

## EPISODE FIVE: "DRAGLEXA"

In the mini challenge, the queens team up and participate in RuPaul's Dog Race. Krystal Versace and Scarlett Harlett emerge as the victorious pair. As for the main challenge of the week, the teams are tasked with marketing their own in-home smart assistant named Draglexa. Due to their mini challenge win, Krystal Versace and Scarlett Harlett are chosen as the team captains.

Team Krystal Versace consists of Krystal herself, along with Charity Kase, River Medway, and Vanity Milan. On the other hand, Team Scarlett Harlett comprises Scarlett herself, Choriza May, Ella Vaday, and Kitty Scott-Klaus.

On the runway, the queens showcase their extravagant drag looks under the category of "Ex-Penny Henny" (Expensive-looking drag). Once both teams' commercials are revealed, RuPaul expresses disappointment, stating that neither commercial was impressive enough for anyone to win the challenge this week.

Charity Kase, Scarlett Harlett, and Vanity Milan find themselves in the bottom three, with Vanity Milan being spared from elimination. Charity Kase and Scarlett Harlett then engage in a lip-sync battle to the song "Big Spender" by Shirley Bassey. Scarlett Harlett comes out on top, winning the lip-sync, while Charity Kase sashays away from the competition.

**Departure Message:** "See you in your Nightmares skanks! I love you all. Charity Kase"

## QUEEN PROFILE: CHARITY KASE

Charity Kase, whose real name is Harry Whitfield was born and raised in Rufford, Lancashire. Whitfield displayed a passion for design and makeup from an early age. During their teenage years, they explored their creative inclinations by donning costumes and making appearances in Liverpool and Manchester.

In their career, Charity Kase was employed at the London club called The Box starting from 2018. They gained significant visibility as one of east London's most daring drag queens, amassing hundreds of thousands of followers on Instagram. Known for their extravagant and outrageous looks, Charity Kase partnered with Wildcat Gin in 2021 to promote a new gin flavour.

Charity Kase is considered the "drag daughter" of Raja, who emerged as the winner of the third season of RuPaul's Drag Race in the United States.

Currently, Whitfield is based in London, continuing to showcase their unique drag artistry and make an impact in the entertainment industry.

## GUEST JUDGE PROFILE: LEIGH-ANNE PINNOCK

Leigh-Anne Pinnock, born 4$^{th}$ October 1991, is an English singer and songwriter who gained fame in the 2010s as a member of the British girl group Little Mix. Pinnock's contributions to the group include nineteen top-ten singles, five number-one hits, and six consecutive top-five albums on the UK Albums Chart. Little Mix made history by becoming the first girl group to achieve this and spent a cumulative total of 100 weeks in the top 10 of the UK Singles Chart. Following the group's hiatus in 2022, Pinnock signed with Warner Records.

During her time in Little Mix, Pinnock released the critically acclaimed documentary "Leigh-Anne: Race, Pop & Power" in 2021. The documentary received a nomination for "Best Authored Documentary" at the 26th National Television Awards. She also made her acting debut in the film "Boxing Day" in 2021, which featured an all-black cast, making it the first British festive rom-com to do so. Pinnock is known for her advocacy work, particularly on racial issues and racial equality. Her efforts in this area earned her a National Diversity and Visionary Honour Award for her contributions to racial equality in the UK.

Born to black mixed-race parents, Deborah Thornhill and John Pinnock, Leigh-Anne Pinnock grew up in a Caribbean household in High Wycombe, Buckinghamshire. She has Barbadian and Jamaican ancestry and considers Jamaica her second home. Before joining Little Mix, Pinnock worked as a waitress at Pizza Hut. She developed her singing skills in a youth club and choir led by Jay Blades, who later became a trustee of her charity, The Black Fund, which she founded in 2021. In 2020, Pinnock spoke out about experiencing racism at the age of nine, sharing her story in a documentary aired on Channel 4.

Pinnock draws inspiration from musical icons like Mariah Carey and Rihanna. Throughout her career with Little Mix, she co-wrote over 50 songs and shares songwriting credits on hits such as "Wings" (2012) and "Shout Out to My Ex" (2016), both of which reached number one in the UK. Little Mix's success has made them one of the best-selling girl groups and one of Britain's top-selling acts. In December 2021, the group announced a hiatus following their Confetti Tour in 2022, allowing the members to pursue solo projects.

In February 2022, Pinnock signed a record deal with Warner Records and joined TaP Music for her solo activities. She received numerous accolades for her documentary and activism work, including "Documentary of the Year" at the Visionary Honours Awards and "Media Champion in Public Eye" at the Burberry British Diversity Awards. Pinnock ventured into solo music and released covers on YouTube, performed narration for an audiobook, and announced her memoir titled "Believe," set to be released in October 2023. She continues to be an ambassador for Maybelline New York and has launched her own production company, Pinnock Productions, to promote diversity and underrepresented cultures in the media.

Pinnock is also involved in various endorsements and philanthropic efforts. She co-founded the swimwear range In'A'Seashell, partnered with Umbro as their face, and released a style edit collection with ASOS. Pinnock's charitable work includes climbing Mount Kilimanjaro to raise funds for Comic Relief's Red Nose Day and co-founding The Black Fund alongside her fiancé and sister. She actively advocates for causes such as Black Lives Matter, racial equality, colourism, and feminism. Her documentary shed light on racial issues and colourism in the music industry, earning critical acclaim and several awards.

# EPISODE SIX: "SNATCH GAME"

In this week's mini challenge, the queens engage in some playful reading as part of the challenge. Choriza May emerges as the victor, displaying her wit and humour. Excitement fills the air as the queens are informed that they will be competing in the highly anticipated Snatch Game. Joining the panel of judges are the delightful Judi Love and the talented Nadine Coyle.

The cast for the Snatch Game includes:

- Choriza May as the vibrant and charismatic Margarita Pracatan
- Ella Vaday as the charming and culinary icon Nigella Lawson
- Kitty Scott-Claus as the fabulous and outspoken Gemma Collins
- Krystal Versace as the lovable and eccentric Charity Shop Sue, aka Selina Mosinski
- River Medway as the bubbly and lively Amy Childs
- Scarlett Harlett as the mischievous and unexpected Macaulay Culkin
- Vanity Milan as the energetic and talented Jocelyn Jee Esien

As the queens hit the runway, the theme for the evening is "Feeling Fruity." Ella Vaday and Kitty Scott-Claus impress the judges with their fruity-inspired looks, receiving positive critiques. Ultimately, Ella Vaday shines the brightest, securing the win for the challenge with her impeccable performance.

Unfortunately, not all queens receive the same level of praise. Choriza May, Krystal Versace, and River Medway face criticism from the judges. However, Krystal Versace manages to avoid elimination and is granted another chance to prove herself. Choriza May and River Medway find themselves in the bottom two and must lip-sync for their lives to the iconic song "Shout" by Lulu and The Luvvers.

After an intense lip-sync performance, RuPaul expresses disappointment and decides to eliminate both Choriza May and River Medway from the competition. The journey for these talented queens comes to an end, but their charisma and passion will surely be remembered.

**Choriza May's Departure Message:** "My peach and my heart will always be full of love for you! Os amo sisters! Choriza May "

**River Medway's Departure Message:** "You won girls. Enjoy the badges. I hope you spend it on some lessons in grace and decorum because you have as much grace as a reversing dump truck. Love you all River xxx"

## QUEEN PROFILE: CHORIZA MAY

Choriza May, born Adrian Martín, is a Spanish-British drag performer, graphic designer and illustrator, whose career took off in 2019 when she participated in Drag Idol, a renowned drag competition in the United Kingdom. Her impressive talent and captivating performances led her to the final, where she emerged as the winner, surpassing formidable competitors Pebble Dash and Chanel Marie. As a result of her success, May had the opportunity to perform on the main stage of Northern Pride, further solidifying her presence in the drag scene.

In 2023, Choriza May joined the esteemed panel of judges for Drag Idol UK, an exciting event held at Bobby's in Newcastle. Her expertise and discerning eye contributed to the selection of future drag superstars.

Outside of her drag persona, Choriza May hails from Guadassuar, València, and currently resides in Newcastle, United Kingdom.

While she embraces her Spanish heritage, she also holds British citizenship, representing a fusion of cultures that adds depth and richness to her artistry.

## QUEEN PROFILE: RIVER MEDWAY

Dexter Clift, professionally known as River Medway was born in Medway, Kent, Dexter derived her drag name from the River Medway that flows through her hometown, symbolising her connection to her roots. In 2021, River Medway was unveiled as one of the talented drag queens competing in the highly anticipated third series of RuPaul's Drag Race UK. Her memorable runway look, inspired by Thomas Fletcher Waghorn, garnered significant attention on social media for its comedic flair.

Throughout her journey on the show, River Medway shared a personal and emotional aspect of her life. She opened up about the tragic loss of her mother to COVID-19, revealing that she received the call to join the show shortly after her passing. This profound experience added depth and vulnerability to her performance on the show, earning her a special place in the hearts of viewers.

Sadly, River Medway's time on RuPaul's Drag Race UK came to an end after the Snatch Game episode. Following a lip sync performance to "Shout," RuPaul made the difficult decision to eliminate both River Medway and her fellow contestant, Choriza May, resulting in a double elimination.

In 2022, River Medway embarked on RuPaul's Drag Race UK: The Official Tour, captivating audiences with her talent and charisma alongside her fellow cast members. Additionally, she is set to showcase her skills in the show Death Drop: Back in the Habit, where she will join forces with other Drag Race alumni, including Victoria Scone, Willam Belli, and Cheryl Hole.

## GUEST JUDGE PROFILE: LULU

Lulu Kennedy-Cairns CBE, born Marie McDonald McLaughlin Lawrie 3rd November 1948, is a Scottish singer, actress, and television personality. Renowned for her powerful singing voice, Lulu gained fame not only in the UK but also internationally. She achieved major chart success with songs like "To Sir with Love," which topped the Billboard Hot 100 and was featured in the 1967 film of the same name and the title track to the 1974 James Bond film "The Man with the Golden Gun." Lulu is also known for her winning entry in the 1969 Eurovision Song Contest, "Boom Bang-a-Bang," and her performance of "Shout" at the closing ceremony of the 2014 Commonwealth Games in Glasgow.

Lulu was born in Lennoxtown, Stirlingshire, and grew up in Dennistoun, Glasgow. She attended Thomson Street Primary School and Onslow Drive School. At a young age, she showed her talent as a singer and joined a band called the Bellrocks for stage experience. Her exceptional voice was already evident even then. Lulu received her stage name from her manager Marion Massey when she was just 14 or 15 years old.

In 2017, Lulu's family history was explored in the UK series "Who Do You Think You Are?" revealing interesting details about her maternal grandparents' different religions and the opposition their union faced. Lulu's career took off in 1964 when she signed with Decca Records under the guidance of Marion Massey. Her debut single, a cover of the Isley Brothers' "Shout" credited to "Lulu & the Luvvers," reached No. 7 on the UK chart. She continued to release successful singles like "Leave a Little Love" in 1965 and "The Boat That I Row" in 1967.

After leaving Decca, Lulu signed with Columbia and began working with producer Mickie Most. She achieved more chart success with songs like "Boom Bang-A-Bang," which reached No. 2 in 1969. Lulu also ventured into acting, making her debut in the 1967 film "To Sir, with Love" alongside Sidney Poitier. She not only acted in the film but also performed the title song, which became a major hit in the United States, reaching No. 1 on the charts.

During the late 1960s, Lulu had several television series of her own in the UK. She hosted shows like "Gadzooks! It's The In-Crowd," "Stramash!," and "Three of a Kind." In 1968, she started her own BBC One TV series, which ran until 1975 under various titles. Lulu's TV shows featured music, comedy sketches, and guest appearances.

Lulu represented the United Kingdom in the 1969 Eurovision Song Contest with the song "Boom Bang-a-Bang," which emerged as the winner. Despite her initial reluctance to participate, the song became a huge success. She later hosted the UK's Eurovision qualifying heat, "A Song for Europe," in 1975.

## EPISODE SEVEN: "THE MISS FUGLY BEAUTY PAGEANT"

In this week's main challenge, the talented queens were presented with the exciting task of creating three unique looks for the highly anticipated Miss Fugly Beauty Pageant. The three categories they had to showcase their creativity were Fugly Swimwear, Charity Shop Chic, and Fugly But Fashionable. Adding to the excitement, the queens received valuable advice from none other than the renowned internet personality Charity Shop Sue.

During the runway presentation, Ella Vaday, Kitty Scott-Claus, and Krystal Versace impressed the judges with their exceptional looks, earning them well-deserved positive critiques. Ultimately, it was Kitty Scott-Claus who emerged victorious, capturing the challenge win with her exceptional creativity and style.

Unfortunately, Scarlett Harlett and Vanity Milan found themselves in the bottom two. The lip-sync battle to the iconic tune of "Scandalous" by Mis-Teeq ensued, with both queens giving it their all. In the end, Vanity Milan delivered an outstanding performance, securing her victory in the lip-sync, while Scarlett Harlett sashayed away from the competition.

The competition continues to heat up as the remaining queens showcase their remarkable talents and strive for the coveted title.

**Departure Message:** "My one single talent got me to the TOP 5... Maybe now you'll get a word in Edgeways!! Love you all Scarlett"

## QUEEN PROFILE: SCARLETT HARLETT

Scarlett Harlett, born Harry Mulvany in 1995, is a British drag queen hailing from the Isle of Dogs in East London. Embarking on a career in drag at the tender age of 17, Mulvany found inspiration in the iconic series RuPaul's Drag Race, which sparked his passion for the art form. Since then, Scarlett Harlett has graced stages with incredible performances, captivating audiences with his unique style.

Aside from his drag pursuits, Mulvany has also ventured into the world of film and television. Notably, he has had the opportunity to contribute his talents as an extra in popular productions such as Absolutely Fabulous and Rocketman.

## GUEST JUDGE PROFILE: ALESHA DIXON

Alesha Anjanette Dixon, born 7th October 1978, is a multi-talented English artist known for her skills in singing, rapping, dancing, and television hosting. She gained fame in the early 2000s as a member of the R&B, garage, and hip-hop group Mis-Teeq, which achieved several UK top 10 hits and released two double-platinum albums. After the group disbanded in 2005, Dixon pursued a solo music career, signing with Polydor Records and releasing her debut album "Fired Up" in 2006. Although her popularity as a singer declined after the release of her debut single "Lipstick" and subsequent track "Knockdown," she made a comeback in 2007 by winning the fifth series of BBC One's "Strictly Come Dancing."

Her success on the dance show led to a resurgence in her music career, and she signed with Asylum Records. In 2008, she released her second album, "The Alesha Show," which achieved platinum certification in the UK. The album spawned hit singles such as "The Boy Does Nothing" and "Breathe Slow," the latter earning her a Brit Award nomination and becoming her highest-charting single. Dixon also became a judge on the seventh series of "Strictly Come Dancing" in 2009. The following year, she released her third album, "The Entertainer." In 2012, she left "Strictly Come Dancing" to become a judge on the ITV talent show "Britain's Got Talent." Dixon continued her music career with the release of her fourth album, "Do It for Love," in 2015.

Aside from her music endeavours, Dixon has been a television presenter on shows such as "Alesha's Street Dance Stars," "Your Face Sounds Familiar," "Text Santa," "Dance Dance Dance," "The Greatest Dancer," "Comic Relief," and she even hosted the Eurovision Song Contest in 2023 alongside Julia Sanina and Hannah Waddingham with Graham Norton joining them for the final. She is also an author and has written a series of children's books called "Lightning Girl."

## EPISODE EIGHT: "BRA WARS"

In this week's primary test, the queens are tasked with showcasing their overacting skills in the low-budget film, "Bra Wars - The Fempire Claps Back." Ella Vaday takes on the role of Daft Shader, Kitty Scott-Claus embodies Brabarella, Krystal Versace portrays She-3PHO, and Vanity Milan embraces the character of Baby Yolo.

On the runway, the queens flaunt their Scene Stealer looks, and all receive positive critiques for their outstanding performances. Krystal Versace and Vanity Milan are announced as safe for the week. However, the top two queens of the challenge are revealed to be Ella Vaday and Kitty Scott-Claus. These two talented queens will now engage in a lip-sync battle for the ultimate victory. Their lip-sync song is "Something New" by Girls Aloud. In a surprising twist, Ru declares both Ella Vaday and Kitty Scott-Claus as the winners of the challenge.

## GUEST JUDGE PROFILE: RUSSELL TOVEY

Russell George Tovey, born 14th November 1981, is an accomplished English actor, with notable roles such as Steve in the sitcom "Him & Her," Kevin Matheson in the HBO series "Looking," and Patrick Read in "American Horror Story: NYC."

During his early years, Tovey grew up in Billericay, Essex, and displayed a passion for collecting various items and participating in different trends. His parents supported his interests, taking him to archaeological digs, museums, and even buying him a metal detector. Initially considering a career as a history teacher, Tovey's aspiration shifted towards acting after being inspired by films like "Dead Poets Society," "The Goonies," and "Stand By Me." During his teenage years, he worked as a kitchen assistant in a local pub.

Tovey's acting journey began at a young age when he joined a local drama club and attracted the attention of a talent agent. He started working in the television industry at the age of 11, making appearances in shows like "Mud." Despite missing a significant amount of school due to acting commitments, Tovey's parents supported his pursuit of a career in acting.

After leaving secondary school at 16, Tovey enrolled in a BTEC performing arts course at Barking College. However, he was expelled after a year for prioritising a paying acting job over a school play role. Tovey gained valuable experience performing in plays under the direction of Debra Gillett, and he met playwright Patrick Marber through Gillett, leading to his involvement in productions like "Howard Katz" at the National Theatre.

In 2004, Tovey gained widespread recognition for his role as Rudge in Alan Bennett's play "The History Boys" at the Royal National Theatre. He continued to portray the character in the play's Broadway, Sydney, Wellington, and Hong Kong productions, as well as its radio and film adaptations. Tovey's determination to improve his skills led him to enrol in workshops and readings offered by the National Theatre.

Throughout his career, Tovey has taken on a diverse range of roles in various television shows, films, and stage productions. He played the lovable werewolf George Sands in "Being Human" and had notable appearances in shows like "Rob Brydon's Annually Retentive" and "Doctor Who." Tovey's talent extended to film, with works like "Huge" and appearances in television pilots such as "Him & Her" and "The Increasingly Poor Decisions of Todd Margaret."

In addition to his acting pursuits, Tovey is also involved in writing and art collecting. He has written plays and short stories, and one of his stories was published in a women's magazine. Tovey wrote and sought funding for the short film "Victor." As an art collector, he began his collection at the age of 21 and owns works by renowned artists such as Tracey Emin, Wolfgang Tillmans, and Rose Wylie. Tovey is passionate about supporting emerging and mid-career artists and has curated exhibitions and hosted a podcast called "Talk Art" with gallerist Robert Diament (lead singer of Temposhark)

Tovey's contributions to the arts have been widely recognised, including receiving the Culture Award at the Virgin Atlantic Attitude Awards. He has curated exhibitions and served as a jury member for prestigious events like the Turner Prize. In 2022, Tovey became the patron of the Art UK charity, further solidifying his dedication to the art world.

# EPISODE NINE: "THE PEARLY GATES ROAST"

In this week's main challenge, the queens are tasked with delivering a hilarious roast targeting the judges and eliminated queens from series 3.

As the queens strut down the runway, they showcase their divine looks for the category "Oh My Goddess." Each queen receives exceptional feedback for their runway presentations. Ultimately, Ella Vaday is declared the challenge winner, setting her place in the finale. Kitty Scott-Claus is deemed safe, also securing her spot in the finale.

The bottom two queens, Krystal Versace and Vanity Milan, face off in a lip-sync battle to Dua Lipa's "Hallucinate." Krystal Versace delivers an outstanding performance and emerges victorious, securing her spot in the finale alongside Ella and Kitty. Unfortunately, it's the end of the road for Vanity Milan, as she sashays away after finding herself in the bottom two for the fourth time.

**Departure Message:** "I came I saw I conquered! Vanity"

## QUEEN PROFILE: VANITY MILAN

Christopher Adamson, professionally known as Vanity Milan, is a British drag queen who gained recognition for his appearance on the third series of RuPaul's Drag Race UK. In 2022, he also competed on Canada's Drag Race: Canada vs. the World.

Adamson, who is of British Jamaican heritage, hails from Mitcham, South London. He embarked on his drag journey in 2019, debuting in London's drag scene. Vanity Milan's stage name was inspired by his mother's nickname for him, highlighting his love for fashion. His talented husband takes charge of designing his captivating costumes.

The breakout moment for Vanity Milan came in 2021 when he participated in RuPaul's Drag Race UK, showcasing his exceptional talent. During the show, he won a challenge with his song "BDE" and secured three lip-sync victories, matching the record set by Tayce from Series 2. Despite a strong performance, Vanity Milan faced elimination in the ninth episode, finishing the competition in fourth place. Following his appearance on the show, he openly discussed the need for greater diversity on RuPaul's Drag Race UK.

Building on his success, Vanity Milan released his debut single titled "Miss Milan (Don't Play With Me)" in 2022, followed by a second single called "Pissed." He also made a guest appearance in the music video for Cheryl Hole's debut single, "Need the Power." In addition, Vanity Milan and Kitty Scott-Claus appeared as contestants on an episode of Pointless Celebrities in June 2022.

Later in the same year, Vanity Milan was announced as a participant in Canada's Drag Race: Canada vs. the World. His performance in the first challenge, including a winning lip sync, showcased his talent with the song "Bonjour, Hi." Unfortunately, he was eliminated in the fifth episode, ultimately securing fifth place in the competition.

In his personal life, Adamson moved to Estonia in 2011, residing there for five years. It was during this time that he met his husband, Siim Adamson, an Estonian citizen.

## GUEST JUDGE PROFILE: KATHY BURKE

Katherine Lucy Bridget Burke, known professionally as Kathy Burke, is a highly acclaimed English actress, comedian, writer, producer, and director. Burke was born 13th June 1964 at the Royal Free Hospital in London. She was raised in Islington, North London, by her Irish Catholic parents, Paddy and Bridget, along with her two elder brothers. After attending the Maria Fidelis Convent School, she studied at the Anna Scher Theatre School in Islington.

She gained widespread recognition for her performances in popular sketch shows like French and Saunders (1988-1999) and her recurring role as Magda in the BBC sitcom Absolutely Fabulous (1992-2012). Burke is also known for her collaborations with fellow comedian Harry Enfield. Notably, she received a British Comedy Award and two BAFTA nominations for her portrayal of Linda La Hughes in the BBC sitcom Gimme Gimme Gimme (1999-2001).

Burke's film debut came in 1982 with the drama Scrubbers. She achieved critical acclaim for her role as Valerie in the 1997 film Nil by Mouth, which earned her the Best Actress award at the Cannes Film Festival and a BAFTA nomination. Throughout her career, Burke has appeared in notable films such as Sid and Nancy (1986), Dancing at Lughnasa (1998), Elizabeth (1998), This Year's Love (1999), Kevin & Perry Go Large (2000), The Martins (2001), Anita and Me (2002), Once Upon a Time in the Midlands (2002), Tinker Tailor Soldier Spy (2011), Pan (2015), and Absolutely Fabulous: The Movie (2016).

In the 2010s, after dedicating much of her time to theatre directing, additionally, she hosted a series of documentaries for Channel 4, including Kathy Burke's All Woman (2019), Kathy

Burke: Money Talks (2021), and Kathy Burke: Growing Up (2023), where she explored topics related to modern women, marriage, pregnancy, and cosmetic surgery.

In addition to her acting career, Burke has made significant contributions as a director. She made her directorial debut with the play "Mr Thomas" in 1990 and went on to direct the BBC Three sketch show series Horne & Corden in 2009. She has also written and appeared in various productions, including the autobiographical film "Better Than Christmas" for Sky 1's Little Crackers and the four-part series "Walking and Talking" based on her teenage years.

## EPISODE TEN: "GRAND FINALE"

In the grand finale of the series, the queens are faced with their ultimate challenge: writing, recording, and performing their own verses to RuPaul's festive anthem, "Hey Sis, It's Christmas."

After putting their creative skills to the test, the queens grace the runway for one final time, showcasing their dazzling looks and impeccable style. As the tension builds, it is revealed that all the queens will engage in an epic lip-sync battle to the iconic tune "You Don't Own Me" by Dusty Springfield.

As the performances unfold, the judges deliberate, and the excitement reaches its peak. In a thrilling turn of events, Krystal Versace emerges as the triumphant winner of the challenge, showcasing her exceptional talent and securing her place in drag race history. Meanwhile, Ella Vaday and Kitty Scott-Claus stand out as remarkable runners-up, their journey filled with remarkable achievements and unforgettable moments.

With the final verdict delivered, the stage is set for a grand conclusion to a season filled with talent, charisma, and fierce competition. The queens have left an indelible mark on the show, their passion and dedication shining through every step of the way. The finale promises to be an unforgettable celebration of drag excellence.

## RUNNER UP: ELLA VADAY

Nick Collier, known professionally as Ella Vaday, is an English drag queen, actor, and dancer. Born 23$^{rd}$ September 1988, Collier grew up in Dagenham, East London. With a passion for singing and dancing from a young age, he pursued his artistic aspirations by attending Bird College, a prestigious performing arts school in Sidcup, South East London.

Collier's career took off as a backup dancer for notable artists like Olly Murs and Eoghan Quigg on the popular talent show The X Factor. He also boasts an impressive theatre background, having performed in productions such as Book of Mormon, Cats, Fame, Joseph and the Amazing Technicolor Dreamcoat, Peter Pan, and Wicked. Additionally, Collier has successfully managed a dog walking business alongside his artistic interests.

His portrayal of Nigella Lawson during the Snatch Game challenge garnered praise and was hailed as iconic by Conor Clark of Gay Times. Ella Vaday emerged as one of the three finalists, showcasing her talents in the final lip-sync performance to Dusty Springfield's "You Don't Own Me," alongside Krystal Versace and Kitty Scott-Claus.

Beyond the world of drag, Collier is set to make his appearance as Ella Vaday in the upcoming feature film Sumotherhood, a follow-up project for Adam Deacon, slated for release in November 2023.

In the midst of the COVID-19 pandemic, Ella Vaday experienced a surge in popularity, with her social media following growing from 6,000 to 30,000 followers. This newfound recognition further sets Collier's status as a rising star in the drag and entertainment industry.

## RUNNER UP: KITTY SCOTT-CLAUS

Louis Westwood, professionally known as Kitty Scott-Claus had previously auditioned for the second series of Drag Race UK, displaying her determination to compete on the iconic drag competition.

A notable highlight of Kitty Scott-Claus's journey on the show was her collaboration with Cheryl Hole, a contestant from the first series, as they formed the girl group Gals Aloud. This drag sister duo captivated audiences with their performances and musical prowess.

Throughout the competition, Kitty Scott-Claus demonstrated her versatility and prowess, winning two maxi-challenges in episodes 7 and 8. She maintained a strong performance throughout the season, consistently placing in the top and never finding herself in the bottom placements.

## SERIES THREE WINNER: KRYSTAL VERSACE

Luke Fenn, professionally known as Krystal Versace, born 10$^{th}$ October 2001. At the age of 19, Krystal became the youngest winner in the history of the Drag Race franchise. Hailing from Tunbridge Wells in Kent, she proudly represents her Greek Cypriot heritage, making her the first descendant of Cypriots to compete in the franchise.

Krystal Versace discovered her passion for drag at the young age of 13, embarking on a transformative journey that would lead her to greatness. In August 2021, she was announced as one of the twelve talented contestants on the third series of RuPaul's Drag Race UK. Displaying her exceptional skills, Krystal emerged as a frontrunner, winning the first two main challenges of the competition. Notably, she engaged in an exhilarating top two lip sync against Victoria Scone, captivating the audience with their performance of Bonnie Tyler's "Total Eclipse of the Heart."

Throughout the series, Krystal Versace showcased her versatility and resilience. In the ninth episode, she found herself in the bottom two alongside Vanity Milan, yet triumphed in a captivating lip sync to Dua Lipa's "Hallucinate," securing her spot in the top three alongside Ella Vaday and Kitty Scott-Claus. As the final challenge, Krystal, along with her fellow competitors, wrote, recorded, and performed their own verses to a remix of RuPaul's "Hey Sis, It's Christmas." Demonstrating her exceptional talent and stage presence, she excelled in this pivotal moment.

The climax of Krystal's journey came during the intense lip sync for the crown, where she gave a memorable performance to Dusty Springfield's rendition of "You Don't Own Me." With her undeniable charisma and fierce energy, she emerged as the victor, setting her status as youngest winner to date.

Outside of drag, Luke Fenn, as he prefers to be called, uses he/him pronouns, while in drag, Krystal embraces she/her pronouns. Additionally, Fenn openly shares that he is dyslexic, emphasising the importance of embracing and celebrating diverse experiences and abilities. He attended North Kent College, further nurturing his passion for the performing arts and honing his talents.

Krystal Versace's triumph on RuPaul's Drag Race UK is a testament to her exceptional artistry, determination, and charisma. She has undoubtedly left an indelible mark on the drag world, inspiring future generations of performers to embrace their uniqueness and pursue their dreams with unapologetic passion.

| Contestant | Age | Hometown | Outcome |
|---|---|---|---|
| Krystal Versace | 19 | Royal Tunbridge Wells, England | Winner |
| Ella Vaday | 32 | Dagenham, England | Runner-up |
| Kitty Scott-Claus | 29 | Birmingham, England | Runner-up |
| Vanity Milan | 29 | South London, England | 4th place |
| Scarlett Harlett | 26 | East London, England | 5th place |
| Choriza May | 30 | Newcastle upon Tyne, England | 6th place |
| River Medway | 22 | Medway, England | 6th place |

| Charity Kase | 24 | Rufford, England | 8th place |
| --- | --- | --- | --- |
| Veronica Green | 35 | Rochdale, England | 9th place |
| Victoria Scone | 27 | Cardiff, Wales | 10th place |
| Elektra Fence | 29 | Burnley, England | 11th place |
| Anubis | 19 | Brighton, England | 12th place |

*Information correct at time of filming*

# RUPAUL'S DRAG RACE UK SERIES 4

The official Instagram page of the show announced on 27th of October 2021 that casting for Series 4 was now open, with a deadline and casting close date of 10th of November 2021. The first celebrity guest judge confirmed for the fourth series was Hannah Waddingham, known for her role in Sex Education. Waddingham revealed her appearance on the show during an episode of Jimmy Kimmel Live!, where RuPaul was the guest host. In an interview with Graham Norton in Gay Times, it was revealed that the competitors in the fourth series were some of the best queens seen on the show. Norton mentioned that the season had more freedom compared to the previous one affected by COVID-19.

The fourth season was confirmed to be part of the autumn schedule and was expected to begin airing in September. Guest judges for the season included Mel B, Alison Hammond, Tess Daly, Dame Joanna Lumley, Boy George, Leomie Anderson, Olly Alexander, FKA Twigs, Lorraine Pascale, and Giovanni Pernice as the resident choreographer. Aisling Bea also made a cameo appearance during the comedy challenge.

The premiere date for the fourth series was set for 22nd of September 2022. The show became one of the network's most successful shows, with 51 million stream requests in the UK by September 2022.

The competitors for the fourth series were revealed on 7th of September 2022 and included Dakota Schiffer, the first openly transgender contestant in the British version of the show. RuPaul was absent in the seventh episode, with Michelle Visage taking his place as the main judge and host and Raven joining the judging panel. This marked the first episode RuPaul missed across all the Drag Race franchises hosted by him. Coincidentally, Raven became the first former Drag Race contestant to judge on a RuPaul-fronted franchise.

## EPISODE ONE: "ST4RT YOUR ENGINES"

A dozen fresh queens sashay into the werkroom. The Spice Girls' iconic Olympics performance inspires their first mini-challenge, a thrilling photo shoot. Black Peppa dazzles and snatches the win. The main challenge demands the competitors to strut down the runway with two distinct looks: "BBC Keeping It 100," commemorating the BBC's centennial anniversary, and "Ru Are You?" allowing them to showcase their personal style. During the "BBC Keeping It 100" segment, the queens cleverly reference various beloved BBC shows and characters:

- Baby as Rastamouse
- Black Peppa as Mr Blobby
- Cheddar Gorgeous as BBC Test Card F
- Copper Topp as Julie Walters in the Two Soups sketch
- Dakota Schiffer as Anne Boleyn in Horrible Histories
- Danny Beard as Mr Blobby
- Jonbers Blonde as Blue Peter
- Just May as The Queen Victoria bust from EastEnders
- Le Fil as Pudsey Bear
- Pixie Polite as Del Boy
- Sminty Drop as Antiques Roadshow
- Starlet as Patsy Stone

On the runway, Black Peppa, Sminty Drop, and Starlet receive glowing critiques, ultimately granting Peppa the well-deserved victory. However, Copper Topp secured a safe position despite mixed feedback. Dakota Schiffer and Just May face negative critiques, leading to a lip-sync showdown to the tune of "Let Them Know" by Mabel. Dakota Schiffer outshines May in the lip sync, securing her stay in the competition while May sashays away.

**Departure Message:** "It was gonna be MAY! Love you all x."

## QUEEN PROFILE: JUST MAY

Pete May is originally from Harwich, Essex, England - Just May has honed her craft in the vibrant drag scene, immersing herself in the art of transformation, fashion, and performance. Her journey on RuPaul's Drag Race UK offers a platform for her to showcase her talents, pushing boundaries, and entertain audiences.

Just May, a British drag performer, derived her drag name from a clever play on words. "May" represents both her surname and the month she was born in. Initially, she went by "May" until a memorable competition moment. When asked for her name, she responded with "May, just May," creating a playful and memorable moniker that stuck with her ever since.

As a drag queen, Just May embraces a fluidity of pronouns. In drag, she identifies as She/They, while out of drag, He/They are her preferred pronouns. This reflects her commitment to self-expression and inclusivity, allowing her to navigate the boundaries of gender and challenge traditional norms.

## GUEST JUDGE PROFILE: DAME JOANNA LUMLEY

Dame Joanna Lumley, born on 1st May 1946, is a British actress, presenter, former model, author, television producer, and activist. She is best known for her role as Patsy Stone in the BBC sitcom Absolutely Fabulous, for which she has won two BAFTA TV Awards. Lumley has also received accolades for her work in theatre, including a nomination for the Tony Award for Best Featured Actress in a Play. In addition to her acting career, Lumley is an advocate for various causes, including human rights, animal welfare, and charity.

Lumley's notable television credits include The New Avengers, Sapphire & Steel, Sensitive Skin, Jam & Jerusalem, and Finding Alice. She has also appeared in films such as On Her Majesty's Secret Service, Shirley Valentine, James and the Giant Peach, The Wolf of Wall Street, and Absolutely Fabulous: The Movie. Throughout her career, she has been involved in activism and has supported organisations like Survival International, the Gurkha Justice Campaign, Compassion in World Farming, and Vegetarians' International Voice for Animals.

Born in Srinagar, Jammu and Kashmir, Lumley has had a diverse upbringing. Her father served in the British Indian Army, and she spent part of her childhood in Asia. Lumley pursued a career in modelling before transitioning into acting. She gained fame for her role as Purdey in The New Avengers and later became known for her portrayal of Patsy Stone in Absolutely Fabulous. Lumley's distinctive voice has also led to her work as a voice-over artist.

In addition to her on-screen work, Lumley has been involved in various media projects. She has appeared in advertisements, hosted television shows, and contributed to radio programs. Lumley has also authored her autobiography, titled "No Room for

Secrets." Her passion for travel has led her to host travel documentaries, including series focused on the Nile, Greece, Japan, and the Silk Road.

Lumley's activism is an integral part of her life. She has been a vocal supporter of the Gurkha Justice Campaign, advocating for the rights of Gurkha veterans. Lumley has also been involved in raising awareness about the Tibetan people, the Khonds indigenous people of India, and the Prospect Burma charity. Her advocacy work reflects her personal connection to these causes, as her father served in the Gurkhas during World War II.

Dame Joanna Lumley was recognised for her contributions to drama, entertainment, and charity and was awarded the title of Dame (DBE) in the 2022 New Year Honours. Her talent, activism, and philanthropy have made her a respected figure in the entertainment industry.

# EPISODE TWO: "YASS-TONBURY FESTIVAL"

In this week's main challenge, the queens are tasked with writing, recording, and performing verses to the song "Come Alive" for the Yass-tonbury Festival, a playful parody of the renowned Glastonbury Festival. Leading the teams are Black Peppa and Dakota Schiffer, who earned the positions of team captains due to their victories in last week's challenge and lip sync, respectively.

Black Peppa selects Baby, Jonbers Blonde, Sminty Drop, and Starlet to join her team, known as "The Triple Threats." Meanwhile, Dakota chooses Cheddar Gorgeous, Copper Topp, Danny Beard, Le Fil, and Pixie Polite for her team, aptly named the "Queens of the Bone Age."

On the runway, the theme is "Neon Nights." The "Queens of the Bone Age" emerge as the triumphant team, with Cheddar Gorgeous, Copper Topp, Dakota Schiffer, Danny Beard, Le Fil, and Pixie Polite all excelling in the challenge and claiming victory. Unfortunately, "The Triple Threats" end up as the losing team. Jonbers Blonde, Sminty Drop, and Starlet receive critical feedback, with Sminty managing to secure safety for the week.

Jonbers Blonde and Starlet face off in a lip sync to the tune of "About You Now" by the Sugababes. Ultimately, Jonbers Blonde emerges victorious, while Starlet bids her farewell and sashays away from the competition.

**Departure Message:** "Every fairytale has an ending, but this is only the beginning. Xxx"

## QUEEN PROFILE: STARLET

Starlet (Patrick Pringle), a captivating drag persona, draws inspiration from the glamorous era of old Hollywood. Her drag name is a tribute to her favourite old movie stars, evoking the beauty and elegance of iconic starlets from the past. Marilyn Monroe, Audrey Hepburn, Lana Turner and Grace Kelly with their breathtaking couture and timeless allure.

Starlet embraces femininity and exudes charisma both on and off the stage. When in drag, she prefers the pronouns she/her, fully embodying her glamorous persona. However, when out of drag, Starlet identifies with the pronouns he/him.

Born 6th of May 2000, in Johannesburg, Gauteng, South Africa, Starlet carries the vibrant energy of her birthplace. She later found her way to her hometown of Reigate, Surrey, England, UK. Her diverse background, blending English and South African heritage, adds depth to her artistry and personal experiences.

## GUEST JUDGE PROFILE: FKA TWIGS

Tahliah Debrett Barnett, professionally known as FKA Twigs, is an English singer, songwriter, and dancer. She was born on 16th of January 1988 in Cheltenham, England. At the age of 17, she moved to London and began her career as a backup dancer for various famous musicians. In 2012, she made her musical debut with the release of her EP1.

Her debut studio album, LP1, was released in 2014 and received critical acclaim, reaching high positions on music charts in the UK and the US. She followed it up with the release of the EP M3LL155X in 2015. After a four-year hiatus, she released her second studio album, Magdalene, in 2019. Throughout her career, FKA Twigs has been praised for her genre-bending style, incorporating elements of electronic music, trip hop, R&B, and avant-garde.

Born to an English mother who was a dancer and gymnast and a Jamaican father who was a musician, FKA Twigs grew up in Cheltenham. She attended St Edward's School, where she participated in opera, ballet, and school productions. At the age of 16, she started making music in youth clubs, and at 17, she moved to South London to pursue a career as a dancer. She worked as a backup dancer in music videos for various artists before focusing on her own music career.

FKA Twigs gained recognition for her unique style and distinctive voice. She released several successful singles and collaborated with other artists. Her music videos often feature her own artistic direction and choreography. In addition to her music, FKA Twigs has also ventured into acting, appearing in the film "Honey Boy" and directing music videos.

In 2022, FKA Twigs released the mixtape Caprisongs, which included collaborations with artists such as the Weeknd, Jorja Smith, and Daniel Caesar. She also received the Godlike Genius award at the BandLab NME Awards. In 2023, she released the lead single "Killer" from her upcoming third studio album.

## EPISODE THREE: "NAFF-TA AWARDS"

This week's mini-challenge features the queens voting for a random queen at the Naff-ta Awards. The categories include "Beast in Show," "Best Background Actress in a Non-speaking Role," "Best Scene Stealing Attention Grabbing Camera Hog," "Best Actress Resting on Pretty," and "Best Hot Mess." The winners for each category are as follows: Black Peppa, Copper Topp, Danny Beard, Baby, and Sminty Drop.

For the main challenge, the queens are paired up randomly and tasked with creating a look using the same colours and fabrics. The pairs and their assigned colours are as follows:

- Baby and Dakota Schiffer: Black
- Le Fil and Sminty Drop: Blue
- Black Peppa and Jonbers Blonde: Green
- Cheddar Gorgeous and Copper Topp: Gold
- Danny Beard and Pixie Polite: Purple

On the runway, the category is "Bing-Oh She Better Don't!" Baby, Dakota Schiffer, Le Fil, and Sminty Drop receive positive critiques, and Baby and Dakota emerge as the challenge winners. Black Peppa, Jonbers Blonde, Cheddar Gorgeous, and Copper Topp receive negative critiques. However, Cheddar and Jonbers are deemed safe.

In the lip-sync showdown, Black Peppa and Copper Topp face off to the song "This Is Real" by Jax Jones ft. Ella Henderson. Black Peppa impresses and wins the lip-sync, while Copper Topp sashays away.

**Departure Message:** Love you all so much! Count your lucky stars you won't be playing me at SNATCH GAME - Love Old Maiden xxx

## QUEEN PROFILE: COPPER TOPP

Copper Topp (Simon Wegrzyn), a captivating drag persona, hails from Cheltenham in Gloucestershire, England. With a playful name that combines elegance and a touch of cheekiness.

In drag, Copper Topp embraces the pronouns she/her, fully embodying her fierce persona. Her stage presence is characterised by vibrant energy, impeccable style, and a talent for commanding attention. Outside of drag, Copper Topp embraces the pronouns he/they, showcasing the multifaceted nature of their identity.

Copper Topp left a lasting impression on the competition with a memorable exit quote: "Well, I guess a Topp can bottom." This humorous remark perfectly encapsulates Copper's ability to blend wit, confidence, and vulnerability.

## GUEST JUDGE PROFILE: LEOMIE ANDERSON

Leomie Jasmin Francis Anderson, born 4th February 1993, is a highly accomplished British fashion model, television presenter, and activist. With an impressive career spanning multiple industries, she has made a significant impact in the world of fashion and beyond. Notably, Anderson has graced the catwalks of prestigious fashion shows and gained recognition for her advocacy work.

From Wandsworth, London, and proudly embracing her Jamaican heritage, Anderson embarked on her modelling journey at the age of 14 when she was scouted. Although she initially aspired to become a fashion journalist, fate led her towards the runway. At just 17 years old, she made her mark in the industry by landing her first catwalk show for renowned designer Marc Jacobs, quickly becoming one of his favoured models.

In 2011, Anderson gained further visibility as a participant on Channel 4's reality show, "The Model Agency," which provided an inside look into the world of modelling. Her talent and charisma captured the attention of major fashion brands, leading her to walk for esteemed names such as Giorgio Armani, Burberry, Chloé, Fenty Puma, Tom Ford, Tommy Hilfiger, Calvin Klein, Ralph Lauren, Moschino, Oscar de la Renta, Jeremy Scott, Temperley, Vivienne Westwood, and Yeezy. She also became one of the faces for Rihanna's influential brand, Fenty Beauty, when it launched in 2017. Anderson's campaign portfolio boasts collaborations with renowned makeup artist Pat McGrath, as well as brands like Uniqlo, Topshop, and Jones New York.

Anderson achieved a significant milestone in 2015 when she was selected to walk in the Victoria's Secret Fashion Show. This opportunity propelled her career to new heights, as she went on to participate in the iconic show for four consecutive years. In April 2019, she made history as the sixth Black and first British Black model to become a Victoria's Secret Angel.

Beyond her modelling achievements, Anderson is a passionate advocate for women's rights. In 2016, she launched the LAPP blog (Leomie Anderson, the Project, the Purpose), which later evolved into LAPP Magazine. Through this platform, she aims to foster awareness and discussion surrounding women's mental health, rights, and body consciousness, ultimately promoting female empowerment. Complementing her activism, Anderson founded her own clothing brand, LAPP The Brand, in September 2016. With a focus on women's athletic garments that seamlessly blend fashion and activewear, she empowers women to feel confident and stylish while pursuing an active lifestyle.

Anderson's commitment to promoting positive change extends beyond her written work. She has given inspiring TEDx Talks and has been invited to speak at prestigious institutions like Oxford and Cambridge universities. Furthermore, she has been an outspoken advocate against racial discrimination in the modelling industry, shedding light on the need for inclusivity and diversity.

In April 2021, Anderson expanded her platform by launching her podcast, "Role Model with Leomie Anderson," produced by Somethin' Else and Sony Music. In this series, she engages in insightful conversations with international superstars who are breaking boundaries and shaping culture.

Continuing to captivate audiences with her multifaceted talents, Anderson is set to take on the role of presenter for the popular BBC television series, "Glow Up: Britain's Next Make-Up Star," succeeding Maya Jama, in 2023. This exciting opportunity further solidifies her influence in the world of fashion and television.

Leomie Anderson's career journey exemplifies not only her incredible success as a model but also her unwavering commitment to effecting positive change. With her advocacy work, entrepreneurial ventures, and engaging media projects, Anderson continues to inspire and empower individuals worldwide, leaving an indelible mark on the fashion industry and society as a whole.

# EPISODE FOUR: "CATTY MAN"

For this week's mini-challenge, the queens engage in a spirited game of musical chairs called "Line of Booty Duty," and it is Pixie Polite who emerges as the victorious queen. As a reward, Pixie Polite is given the honour of selecting the teams for the main challenge, which involves improvisation on Alan Carr's show, "Catty Man."

The teams are as follows:

- Cheddar Gorgeous, Danny Beard, and Pixie Polite - Team name: "Curiosity Killed the Katrina"
- Baby, Dakota Schiffer, and Le Fil - Team name: "Kat's Got My Tongue"
- Black Peppa, Jonbers Blonde, and Sminty Drop - Team name: "The Catfish Is Out of the Bag"

On the runway, the queens showcase their creativity in the category "The Mane Event" with the theme "Love Your Hair, Hope You Win." The judges provide positive critiques for Cheddar Gorgeous, Danny Beard, and Pixie Polite, ultimately awarding Danny the challenge win. Unfortunately, Baby, Le Fil, and Sminty Drop receive negative critiques, resulting in Le Fil being declared safe. To determine who will continue in the competition, Baby and Sminty Drop face off in a lip-sync battle, performing to the energetic tune "Respectable" by Mel and Kim. In the end, Baby triumphs in the lip-sync while Sminty Drop gracefully sashays away.

**Departure Message:** The Manchester Mannequin started panicking, but this is NOT the last runway you'll see me on - Sminty

## QUEEN PROFILE: SMINTY DROP

Callum Shaw was born and raised in Clitheroe, Lancashire, England, known as Sminty Drop; she brings her unique style and charisma to the world of drag. With her English heritage, she embraces a diverse cultural background, infusing it with her own artistic flair. Born on 31st of January 1999, Sminty Drop is a young and vibrant queen, adding a fresh perspective to the drag scene.

The name Sminty Drop originated from a memorable night out when Sminty Drop, full of enthusiasm to engage with potential admirers, always carried mints with her to ensure fresh breath. However, being a bit clumsy, she would frequently drop the mints on the floor. Thus, the name Sminty Drop was born, capturing both her love for mints and her endearing clumsiness.

Sminty Drop, a talented performer, embraces a non-binary identity and expresses herself through drag. While in drag, she prefers the pronouns She/Her, as they align with her artistic persona. Outside of drag, she continues to identify as non-binary, using the pronouns She/Her to reflect her personal journey.

## GUEST JUDGE PROFILE: ALISON HAMMOND

Alison Hammond, born 5th of February 1975, is a popular English television personality and actress known for her vibrant personality and charismatic presence. She rose to fame as a contestant on the third series of the reality show Big Brother in 2002, where she captured the hearts of viewers before being evicted as the second housemate. Since then, she has established herself as a versatile presenter and reporter on ITV's This Morning, a widely watched morning television program, where she has been a mainstay since 2002.

Hammond's talent and infectious charm have led to numerous opportunities in the entertainment industry. In 2023, she joined the Channel 4 reality baking competition The Great British Bake Off as a co-presenter, adding her unique flair to the beloved show. Her dynamic presence has also graced various reality shows, including I'm a Celebrity...Get Me Out of Here! in 2010, Celebrity Coach Trip in 2012, Strictly Come Dancing in 2014, Celebrity Masterchef in 2014, and I Can See Your Voice from 2021 to 2022. Additionally, Hammond has displayed her acting skills in TV shows like Palace Hill (1988–1990), Doctors (2002), and The Dumping Ground (2016).

Born to Jamaican parents and raised in Kingstanding, a district in north Birmingham, Hammond's upbringing and cultural background have influenced her charismatic persona. She attended Cardinal Wiseman School and discovered her passion for drama at a young age, participating in workshops run by Central Television. Despite facing financial constraints, she persevered in pursuing her dreams, although she was unable to attend drama school. Eventually, Hammond moved to Hall Green in south Birmingham, expanding her horizons and setting the stage for her successful career.

With her magnetic personality, Hammond has become a beloved figure in the entertainment industry. Her engaging presence and relatable charm have endeared her to audiences across the UK.

## EPISODE FIVE: "LAIRY POPPINS: THE RUSICAL"

In this week's mini-challenge, the queens unleash their razor-sharp wit and engage in a fierce reading session. Ultimately, it is Pixie Polite who reigns supreme, earning the victory. For the main challenge, the queens are tasked with showcasing their vocal prowess and performing in the spectacular production of "Lairy Poppins: The Rusical."

Each queen takes on a unique role:

- Baby mesmerizes as Mother
- Black Peppa and Dakota Schiffer bring their talent to life as Daughter
- Cheddar Gorgeous embodies the sassy Cockroach
- Danny Beard captivates the audience as the one and only Lairy Poppins
- Jonbers Blonde enchants as Bird Woman
- Le Fil shines in the iconic role of Mary Poppins
- Pixie Polite charms as the delightful Chimney Sweep

On the runway, the queens strut their stuff to the theme of "West End Wonders." Danny Beard, Jonbers Blonde, and Pixie Polite receive glowing critiques for their exceptional performances, with Danny Beard snatching the well-deserved challenge win. Unfortunately, Baby, Dakota Schiffer, and Le Fil face some criticism during the judging, but Le Fil secures safety for the next round.

As tensions rise, Baby takes a courageous step and announces her departure from the competition, citing mental health issues as the reason behind her decision. Dakota Schiffer, deeply impacted by Baby's departure, is granted safety for the week, allowing her to continue her journey on the show. The lip-sync battle commences as Baby and Dakota Schiffer deliver a mesmerizing performance to the rhythm of "No Way" by The Cast of Six ft. Renée Lamb.

In the wake of the emotional lip-sync, the competition moves forward with the remaining queens, each ready to face the challenges that lie ahead.

**Departure Message:** "Hands up say "Bye Baby" but not for long love you all!!! Xoxo"

## QUEEN PROFILE: BABY

Baby, a charismatic and dynamic drag performer, derived her name from a cherished aspect of her personal history. As the youngest among five siblings, she was affectionately referred to as "the baby." When the opportunity arose to choose a drag name during a spirited lip sync competition at university, Baby embraced her cherished nickname.

With a unique blend of English and Afro-Jamaican heritage, Baby captivates audiences with her vibrant performances and diverse cultural influences. Her artistic expression transcends traditional boundaries, pushing the boundaries of gender and challenging societal norms.

Within the world of drag, Baby shines as a versatile performer, utilising her talent to showcase a wide range of styles and characters. Whether exuding sensuality and grace or commanding the stage with bold charisma, Baby possesses a magnetic presence that captivates all who witness her performances.

Offstage, Baby embraces an inclusive and fluid identity, utilising the pronouns They/Them and He/Him. This acknowledgement of their multifaceted nature extends beyond the glamorous facade, allowing Baby to explore and express the various facets of their identity.

Hailing from South London, England, Baby is deeply influenced by the rich cultural tapestry that surrounds her. This fusion of backgrounds and experiences permeates her artistry, resulting in performances that are vibrant, dynamic, and thought-provoking.

## GUEST JUDGE PROFILE: HANNAH WADDINGHAM

Hannah Waddingham is a highly accomplished English actress renowned for her exceptional talent and versatility. Born on 28th July 1974, she has made a significant impact in both stage and screen performances, garnering critical acclaim and numerous accolades throughout her career.

Waddingham's breakthrough role came with her portrayal of Rebecca Welton in the hit comedy series "Ted Lasso" (2020–2023). Her exceptional performance as Rebecca earned her prestigious awards, including the Primetime Emmy Award for Outstanding Supporting Actress in a Comedy Series in 2021 and the Critics' Choice Television Award for Best Supporting Actress in a Comedy Series in 2021 and 2022.

A true powerhouse on the stage, Waddingham has showcased her talent in a variety of West End productions. She has captivated audiences with her memorable performances in shows like "Spamalot," "Into the Woods," and "The Wizard of Oz," earning her three Olivier Award nominations.

In addition to her theatrical accomplishments, Waddingham has made significant contributions to the screen. She appeared in the acclaimed film adaptation of "Les Misérables" (2012) and joined the cast of the HBO series "Game of Thrones" in its fifth season, portraying the unforgettable character Septa Unella. She co-starred in the 2018 British psychological thriller Winter Ridge, directed by Dom Lenoir, and has had a supporting role in the series Sex Education since 2019. In 2023, she co-hosted the Eurovision Song Contest (along with Graham Norton)

Waddingham's talent extends beyond acting, as she possesses a remarkable four-octave vocal range. Her singing prowess has been showcased in various productions, including her own performances in "Ted Lasso" and the Andrew Lloyd Webber and Ben Elton musical "The Beautiful Game."

Fluent in French and Italian, Waddingham is a true lover of languages. Her dedication to her craft, linguistic abilities, and unwavering commitment to authenticity have solidified her status as a respected and admired figure in the entertainment industry.

As Hannah Waddingham continues to captivate audiences with her extraordinary talent, it is evident that her contributions to the world of acting and performance will continue to leave an indelible mark on the hearts and minds of viewers around the globe.

## EPISODE SIX: "STRICTLY COME SNATCH GAME"

In this week's main challenge, the queens will take part in the Snatch Game. AJ Odudu and Tess Daly are the guest judges for the episode. The talented cast includes:

- Black Peppa as Lil Nas X
- Cheddar Gorgeous as Queen Elizabeth I
- Dakota Schiffer as Pete Burns
- Danny Beard as Cilla Black
- Jonbers Blonde as Saint Patty
- Le Fil as Marie Kondo
- Pixie Polite as Dame Shirley Bassey

On the runway, the theme is Tickled Pink. Both Cheddar Gorgeous and Jonbers Blonde receive positive critiques, with Cheddar Gorgeous ultimately winning the challenge. Unfortunately, Black Peppa, Le Fil, and Pixie Polite face negative critiques, although Pixie Polite is declared safe. Black Peppa and Le Fil find themselves in the bottom two and must lip-sync for their lives to the song "Stop" by Spice Girls. In an intense battle, Black Peppa emerges victorious, while Le Fil sashays away from the competition.

**Departure Message:** Keep whippin' that hair, smash those gender roles! Love, Le Fil-osofical

## QUEEN PROFILE: LE FIL

Le Fil (Philip Li) is a British-Chinese pop artist, singer, and performer from Brighouse in Huddersfield. His music and art blend together as "pop sculpture," exploring gender and identity. He has appeared on magazine covers and toured worldwide, sharing the stage with Melanie C. Often compared to Lady Gaga and Kylie Minogue, his shows are part-concert, part-live art. Le Fil is an activist for LGBTQ+ rights, collaborating with global brands and spreading his vision for equality. He has worked with British Vogue, Toyota, Smirnoff, and many others. His unique perspective challenges gender and genre expectations, transforming imaginations.

## GUEST JUDGE PROFILE: MEL B

Melanie Janine Brown, also known as Mel B or Melanie B, is an English singer, songwriter, TV personality, and actress. She gained fame in the 90s as a member of the Spice Girls, where she was nicknamed Scary Spice. The group became the best-selling female group ever, with over 100 million records sold worldwide. Mel B was born in Leeds, UK, and grew up in the Kirkstall area. She studied performing arts before entering the entertainment industry.

Mel B launched her solo career in 1998 with the hit single "I Want You Back," which topped the UK Singles Chart. She released her debut solo album "Hot" in 2000, followed by the album "L.A. State of Mind" in 2005. In 2013, after an eight-year break, she released the single "For Once in My Life," which reached number 2 on the Billboard Hot Dance Club Songs chart.

Beyond music, Mel B established herself as a TV personality and talent show judge. She appeared on "Dancing with the Stars" in 2007, finishing in second place. She served as a judge on "The X Factor" in Australia and the UK, co-presented "Dancing with the Stars" in Australia, and judged on "America's Got Talent." Mel B also co-presented "Lip Sync Battle UK" and participated in various other TV shows and projects.

## EPISODE SEVEN: "QUEEN TEAM MAKEOVERS"

This week, the queens will undertake the main challenge of giving a drag makeover to a member of the production's Queen Team. On the main stage, they will showcase their transformations for the judges.

On the runway, the theme is "Family Resemblance." Cheddar Gorgeous and Danny Beard impress the judges and receive positive critiques, but it is Cheddar Gorgeous who emerges as the winner of the challenge. Meanwhile, Dakota Schiffer, Jonbers Blonde, and Pixie Polite face criticism for their makeovers. Jonbers Blonde manages to secure safety for the week.

Dakota Schiffer and Pixie Polite find themselves in the bottom two and must lip-sync for their lives to the song "Miss Me Blind" by Culture Club. After a captivating performance, Pixie Polite emerges as the victor of the lip-sync, while Dakota Schiffer sashays away from the competition.

**Departure Message:** "The Doll may have left this valley, but she certainly left her mark! TRANS RIGHTS!"

## QUEEN PROFILE: DAKOTA SCHIFFER

Astrid Basson, professionally known as Dakota Schiffer was born on 21st December 1999, Dakota Schiffer hails from West Sussex, England. Throughout her childhood and adolescence, she faced bullying due to her perceived femininity. Dakota Schiffer identifies as a trans woman and is openly queer. At the age of 15, she came out as queer alongside her non-binary identical twin.

From a young age, Dakota Schiffer developed a passion for fashion and makeup, which eventually led her to discover the world of drag. She pursued higher education at University College London, where she studied geography.

In a historic move, Dakota Schiffer became the first trans contestant to participate in RuPaul's Drag Race UK. Despite landing in the bottom two during the first episode, she triumphed in the lip sync battle against her fellow contestant, Just May. Her standout runway look in the second episode drew inspiration from the world of Pokémon, earning her a challenge win. Dakota Schiffer continued to showcase her talent and secured another challenge victory in the third episode. However, her journey on the show came to an end in week 7 following a lip sync against Pixie Polite.

## GUEST JUDGE PROFILE: RAVEN

David Petruschin, known by his stage name Raven, is an influential American drag queen, renowned makeup artist, and reality television personality hailing from Riverside, California. Prior to gaining international recognition on RuPaul's Drag Race and RuPaul's Drag Race All Stars, Raven established herself as a prominent figure in the Southern California nightclub scene. Despite finishing as the runner-up in both seasons she competed in, Raven left an indelible mark on the show and its audience. Additionally, she served as a "professor" on all three seasons of RuPaul's Drag U, offering mentorship and makeovers to female contestants.

Born on the 8th of April 1979, Raven's upbringing took place in Idaho as the eldest child with Russian ancestry; she was raised in a Mormon household by her mother, who separated from her father when Raven was seven years old.

Before venturing into drag, Petruschin worked as a cosmetics salesperson and a freelance makeup artist, catering to local theatre productions during the day while moonlighting as a go-go boy named "Phoenix" in nightclubs. Raven's debut as a drag performer occurred on 10th of May 2002, when she took the stage alongside Mayhem Miller, who would also go on to participate in RuPaul's Drag Race.

Raven first appeared on RuPaul's Drag Race during its second season in 2010. Despite finding herself in the bottom two in the second and third episodes, she showcased her lip-sync prowess and won both battles. Raven's impeccable fashion sense and skills earned her victories in several mini-challenges throughout the season, setting her presence as a formidable competitor. Ultimately, she finished as the runner-up behind Tyra Sanchez.

Continuing her involvement in the franchise, Raven played a vital role in the spin-off series RuPaul's Drag U, serving as a mentor and "drag professor" to female participants seeking makeovers. Her nurturing and supportive persona endeared her to the audience, earning her the title of the "Makeover Queen" after achieving the most wins in the show's history. Notably, in one episode of the second season, she gave her mother, DeShawna, a makeover, triumphing over Jujubee and Manila Luzon's sisters.

Raven's talent and charisma secured her a spot on the inaugural season of RuPaul's Drag Race: All Stars in 2012. Teamed up with her best friend Jujubee as "Team Rujubee," they excelled in various challenges, winning mini-challenges and securing a place in the final episode. Once again, Raven finished as the runner-up, with Chad Michaels claiming the victory.

Following her on-screen appearances, Petruschin continued working behind the scenes as RuPaul's makeup artist, commencing from the ninth season of Drag Race. His exceptional contributions earned him recognition, including a Primetime Emmy Award in 2020 for Outstanding Makeup for a Multi-Camera

Series or Special (Non-Prosthetic). Additionally, he took on the role of creative producer for both RuPaul's Drag Race and RuPaul's Drag Race All Stars, further showcasing his artistic talents and expertise.

Raven's influence extends beyond the realm of drag. She made notable appearances in commercials, music videos, and television shows, including a cameo on America's Next Top Model. Alongside Raja, another Drag Race winner, Raven co-hosted the popular YouTube fashion critique show "RuPaul's Drag Race Fashion Photo RuView" and has made appearances on various other World of Wonder shows.

Recognised for her distinct style and artistry, Raven's impact on drag fashion has been celebrated. In Vanity Fair's "100 Years of Drag Fashion" video, she was highlighted as a significant inspiration alongside iconic figures like Divine, David Bowie, and RuPaul. Her signature makeup became a defining aspect of contemporary drag, even influencing RuPaul's original makeup artist, Mathu Andersen. Raven's contributions to the drag community have left an enduring legacy, inspiring and influencing countless young drag queens, including Bianca Del Rio, the winner of RuPaul's Drag Race season six.

## GUEST JUDGE PROFILE: BOY GEORGE

George Alan O'Dowd, professionally known as Boy George, is an English singer, songwriter, and DJ. He gained fame as the lead singer of the pop band Culture Club, known for their soulful music and Boy George's androgynous style. Born on 14th of June 1961, in Kent, England, Boy George grew up in Eltham and was influenced by the New Romantic movement of the late 1970s and early 1980s. His unique fashion sense was inspired by glam rock icons David Bowie and Marc Bolan. In 1981, he formed Culture

Club with Roy Hay, Mikey Craig, and Jon Moss. The band achieved great success with their second album, "Colour by Numbers," which sold over 10 million copies worldwide. Their hit singles include "Do You Really Want to Hurt Me," "Karma Chameleon," and "Time (Clock of the Heart)."

In addition to his work with Culture Club, Boy George pursued a solo career starting in 1987. He has released numerous studio albums, singles, and DJ albums throughout his career. Some of his popular solo songs include "Everything I Own," "Generations of Love," and "Love Is Leaving." Boy George's music spans various genres, including pop, new wave, soul, soft rock, disco, and reggae.

Aside from music, Boy George has engaged in various activities such as songwriting, DJing, fashion design, and photography. In January 2016, Boy George became a mentor on the fifth series of The Voice UK, taking over from Tom Jones. One of his notable acts, Cody Frost, achieved a third-place finish. After completing a single season, Boy George departed from the show and later joined The Voice Australia as a coach for its sixth season, replacing The Madden Brothers. His last contestant, Hoseah Partsch, emerged as the runner-up. Boy George made a comeback for the show's seventh season in 2018, its eighth season in 2019 (where his final contestant, Diana Rouvas, won the competition), and its ninth season in 2020. However, he did not participate in the tenth season.

He has also made appearances on television shows and was a contestant on the UK series of "I'm a Celebrity...Get Me Out of Here!" in 2022. Boy George has received numerous awards for his contributions to music, both as a solo artist and as a member of Culture Club.

Despite the ups and downs, Boy George and Culture Club have had several reunions over the years, performing together and releasing new music. They have toured internationally and continue to delight fans with their music. Boy George's influence on the music industry and his unique style have made him a beloved and iconic figure in pop culture.

# EPISODE EIGHT: "THE SQUIRREL GAMES"

In this week's main challenge, the queens are tasked with showcasing their overacting skills in the murder mystery movie "The Squirrel Games." Black Peppa takes on the role of Bev Growls, Cheddar Gorgeous portrays Minxie, Danny Beard embodies Divine-Ah Dickall, Jonbers Blonde tackles the characters of both Sassy and Fugly the Dog, and Pixie Polite portrays Kimmy Booburn.

On the runway, the queens strut their stuff in the "Ruff and Ready" category. Cheddar Gorgeous and Danny Beard impress the judges, earning positive critiques, and it is Cheddar Gorgeous who emerges as the challenge winner. However, Black Peppa and Jonbers Blonde received negative critiques, landing them in the bottom two.

In a surprising twist, Black Peppa and Jonbers Blonde deliver an exceptional lip-sync performance to "Some Kinda Rush" by Booty Luv. Their captivating performance leaves the judges unable to choose a clear winner, resulting in both queens being declared winners of the lip-sync. As a result, no queen is eliminated this week.

## GUEST JUDGE PROFILE: LORRAINE PASCALE

Lorraine Pascale, born on 17th of November 1972, is a British television cook, USA Food Network host, former top model, and successful author. She is widely recognised for her bestselling books, with nearly one million copies sold in the UK alone, and her TV shows have reached audiences in 70 countries worldwide. Pascale had her own cooking show on the BBC for multiple seasons, showcasing her culinary expertise. Additionally, she previously owned Ella's Bakehouse, a popular retail outlet in

London specialising in baked goods, named after her daughter. Pascale is known for her work as the United Kingdom Government Fostering and Adoption Ambassador and her advocacy for emotional wellness. Notably, she is the mother of Ella Balinska, who starred in the film "Charlie's Angels."

Pascale was born in Hackney, London, to Caribbean parents. Shortly after her birth, she was fostered in Leytonstone and later adopted at 18 months old. She was raised in Witney, Oxfordshire, by her adoptive parents.

At the age of 16, Pascale was discovered by an agent who had previously found Naomi Campbell, leading her to pursue a successful career as a model. She walked the runway with renowned supermodels like Naomi Campbell, Karen Mulder, and Kate Moss for prestigious fashion houses such as Chanel and Versace. Pascale achieved a significant milestone as the first black British model to grace the cover of American Elle magazine. She also appeared in the 1998 Sports Illustrated swimsuit issue and starred as one of the "Bond Girls" in Robbie Williams' music video for "Millennium."

Recognising the need to secure her future beyond modelling, Pascale explored various career opportunities, including hypnotherapy and car mechanics. In 2005, she enrolled in a diploma cookery course at Leith's School of Food and Wine, discovering her passion for cooking. After completing her diploma, Pascale gained practical experience by working in several London restaurants. However, she realised that the demanding hours of the restaurant industry would not suit her lifestyle. Instead, Pascale focused on becoming a specialist cakemaker and secured a contract with Selfridges, a renowned department store in London. Her collaboration with Selfridges began at the recommendation of esteemed chef Marco Pierre

White. In 2008 and 2010, Pascale supplied over 1000 Christmas cakes to the store. Additionally, she opened her own cupcake shop in Covent Garden. Pascale further pursued her culinary education by studying Culinary Arts at Thames Valley University (now University of West London), graduating with a first-class degree in March 2012.

In 2011, Pascale embarked on her television career, hosting the bakery program "Baking Made Easy" on BBC television. The show's success led to the publication of a book based on the series. Later that year, she presented a second series called "Home Cooking Made Easy" and released an accompanying cookbook. In 2012, Pascale published another book, "Fast, Fresh & Easy Food," which inspired a TV series of the same name aired on BBC Two. She co-presented and judged the UK version of "My Kitchen Rules" alongside Jason Atherton in 2014. In 2015, Pascale co-hosted an episode of "The Nation's Favourite Food" on BBC Two, appearing alongside the Hairy Bikers.

Pascale's television career extended to the United States, where she served as a judge on Food Network's "Holiday Baking Championship" and "Spring Baking Championship" from 2014 to 2020. She also mentored contestants on "Worst Bakers in America." Additionally, Pascale appeared as a judge on two episodes of the first season of "Bakers vs. Fakers" and eventually became the host for the show's second season before its cancellation in 2017

## EPISODE NINE: "COMEDY QUEENS"

In this week's primary challenge, the queens are tasked with delivering a comedic roast aimed at the judges and the eliminated queens from season 4.

On the runway, the theme is "Pretty in Punk." After the deliberation, it is revealed that Danny Beard is the winner of the challenge, securing her place in the finale. Cheddar Gorgeous and Jonbers Blonde are deemed safe, also earning their spots in the finale. However, Black Peppa and Pixie Polite find themselves in the bottom two and must lip-sync for their lives to the song "Another One Bites the Dust" by Queen. Ultimately, Black Peppa emerges as the victor of the lip-sync, securing the final spot in the finale, while Pixie Polite sashays away.

**Departure Message:** "You're a fabulous top 4 - BUT #pixiewozrobbed! Very Rude!"

## QUEEN PROFILE: PIXIE POLITE

Mark James Dudley Wickens, better known by his stage name Pixie Polite. During the first episode of the season, Pixie paid tribute to the BBC comedy Only Fools and Horses, showcasing a drag ensemble inspired by Del Boy, along with a second look featuring clouds and rays of sunshine. In the Snatch Game challenge, Pixie impersonated the legendary Shirley Bassey.

Throughout the competition, Pixie eliminated Dakota Schiffer and ultimately secured a fifth-place finish in the semi-finals. Following the conclusion of Drag Race, Pixie Polite embarked on a tour alongside the other series 4 contestants. In 2022, Pixie Polite released their debut single titled "Give It To Ya," accompanied by a music video.

Outside of drag, Pixie Polite is based in Brighton and uses he/they pronouns. However, when in drag, she prefers she/her pronouns. Additionally, Pixie Polite was in a relationship with Tia Kofi for approximately five years, and both were members of the group The Vixens.

## GUEST JUDGE PROFILE: OLLY ALEXANDER

Oliver Alexander Thornton, born 15th July 1990, is a renowned British singer and actor. He gained fame as the lead vocalist of the band Years & Years and for his outstanding performance as Ritchie Tozer in the Channel 4 drama series "It's a Sin." Alexander has received six nominations for the Brit Awards and has also been recognised with nominations for the British Academy Television Award for Best Actor and the Critics' Choice Television Award for Best Actor in a Limited Series or Movie Made for Television.

Alexander was born in Harrogate, North Yorkshire. His mother, Vicki Thornton, was one of the founders of the Coleford Music Festival. He attended St John's Primary School in Coleford and later Monmouth Comprehensive School. During his time at Monmouth Comprehensive School, he showcased his acting skills in two school plays: "Guys and Dolls," where he portrayed Benny, and "The Caucasian Chalk Circle," where he played the Corporal. After completing his GCSEs, he pursued Performing Arts at Hereford College of Arts. At the age of 10, Alexander wrote his first song on his father's Casio keyboard.

At the age of 16, Alexander secured an agent while auditioning for a role in the British TV series "Skins." He made the decision to drop out of Hereford College of Arts to pursue his acting career as opportunities started arising. Reflecting on his journey, Alexander stated that he initially aspired to be a singer or musician but unexpectedly found himself pursuing acting. He admitted to having a difficult time in school due to bullying but found solace and acceptance in drama class. Alexander has been candid about his experiences with bullying, bulimia, and mental health challenges in various interviews.

Alexander's acting career began with the release of the film "Summerhill" in 2008. He then appeared in the critically acclaimed film "Bright Star," which received an Academy Award nomination for Best Achievement in Costume Design. He further showcased his acting skills in films like "Tormented" and "Enter the Void" released in 2009. In 2010, he played Evan in the Bush Theatre production of "The Aliens." Alexander also contributed to the script and music of the indie film "The Dish & the Spoon" released in 2011. In 2012, he took on the role of Naz in the theatre production of "Mercury Fur" at The Old Red Lion in Islington.

From March to June 2013, Alexander portrayed Peter Pan in the West End play "Peter and Alice," alongside Ben Whishaw and Judi Dench. He also had a supporting role in the final series of "Skins," appearing as Cassie Ainsworth's stalker in the two-part episode "Skins Pure." Additionally, he made an appearance as a demanding shopper in a Google Analytics internal corporate video.

In 2014, Alexander played a main character in the musical feature film "God Help the Girl," where he showcased his singing and guitar-playing abilities. He also appeared in the film adaptation of Laura Wade's stage play "Posh," titled "The Riot Club," and had a brief portrayal of the vampire Fenton in the series "Penny Dreadful." In 2015, he starred in the indie film "Funny Bunny."

Alexander has received recognition for his talents, receiving nominations for prestigious awards such as the Critics' Choice Television Award for Best Actor in a Limited Series or Movie Made for Television and the British Academy Television Award for Best Actor for his role as Ritchie Tozer in It's a Sin.

# EPISODE TEN: "GRAND FINALE"

In the ultimate test of their skills, the remaining queens are tasked with writing and recording their own verses for a Mega Mix of RuPaul's iconic songs. Following a breathtaking showcase on the Grand Finale Eleganza runway, Black Peppa and Jonbers Blonde face elimination, narrowing down the competition to the final two: Cheddar Gorgeous and Danny Beard. With their hearts racing, they engage in a thrilling lip-sync battle to Shirley Bassey's "This Is My Life." The moment of truth arrives as Danny Beard is crowned the victor, securing the title, while Cheddar Gorgeous gracefully takes the position of the runner-up.

## QUEEN PROFILE: BLACK PEPPA

Akeem Adams, known by their stage name Black Peppa was born in Saint Martin but later relocated to Birmingham in 2014. Black Peppa made their mark with the release of their debut single, "Why Is She Calling?" in November 2022.

Black Peppa identifies as non-binary and queer, embracing their Black heritage. Mo Heart serves as Black Peppa's drag mother. Their drag name, as mentioned by Entertainment Weekly, draws inspiration from both the popular TV series Peppa Pig and the flavourful Caribbean dishes prepared by their mother.

## QUEEN PROFILE: JONBERS BLONDE

Andrew Glover, widely known by their stage name Jonbers Blonde, is a versatile drag performer, model, and entertainer from Belfast, Northern Ireland. As a model and entertainer, Glover captivates audiences with their drag persona, Jonbers Blonde (previously known as JonBenet Blonde). They have made notable contributions as a fashion editor and have graced runways in esteemed fashion capitals like London and Paris. Glover has collaborated with esteemed figures such as Nadine Coyle, Sophie Ellis-Bextor, Melanie C, Sam Smith, and Years & Years.

Jonbers Blonde gained prominence by competing on the fourth season of RuPaul's Drag Race UK. Although they did not receive any badges during the competition, they achieved a joint third placement in the finale, showcasing their talent and creativity. Additionally, Jonbers Blonde made a cameo appearance in the series I Hate Suzie.

## RUNNER UP: CHEDDAR GORGEOUS

Cheddar Gorgeous, whose real name is Michael Atkins, is an English drag performer, identifies as non-binary. Prior to their appearance on Drag Race UK, Cheddar Gorgeous had also been featured on Drag SOS.

Originally from Birmingham, Cheddar Gorgeous currently resides in Manchester. Their drag name is inspired by the renowned landmark, Cheddar Gorge. In addition to their drag career, Atkins holds a PhD in Anthropology from the University of Manchester.

In 2023, Cheddar Gorgeous made a guest appearance as a celebrity in the sixth episode of Series 5 of Glow Up: Britain's Next Make-Up Star, which aired on BBC Three.

## SERIES FOUR WINNER: DANNY BEARD

Danny Beard, whose real name is Daniel Curtis (born 27th of May 1992), is a British drag performer and singer from Liverpool.

In 2016, they auditioned for the tenth series of Britain's Got Talent and reached the semi-finals. In 2021, they competed in Karaoke Club: Drag Edition and finished in fourth place.

In 2022, Danny Beard joined the cast of Series 4 of RuPaul's Drag Race UK, becoming the sixth bearded queen in the Drag Race franchise and the first to be judged by RuPaul. Throughout the competition, they won four main challenges, making them the fourth contestant in the history of RuPaul's Drag Race UK to achieve this. They made it to the finale without ever facing elimination. On 24th of November 2022, Danny Beard was announced as the winner of the season, becoming the first bearded winner in any Drag Race franchise.

In March 2023, Danny Beard graced the screens with an appearance in the Channel 4 soap opera, Hollyoaks. Then, in May, they had a delightful cameo in the Eurovision Song Contest 2023, which was hosted in Liverpool on behalf of Ukraine.

| Contestant | Age | Hometown | Outcome |
| --- | --- | --- | --- |
| Danny Beard | 29 | Liverpool, England | Winner |
| Cheddar Gorgeous | 38 | Manchester, England | Runner-up |
| Black Peppa | 29 | Birmingham, England | 3rd |
| Jonbers Blonde | 33 | Belfast, Northern Ireland | 3rd |
| Pixie Polite | 29 | Brighton, England | 5th |
| Dakota Schiffer | 22 | Horsham, England | 6th |
| Le Fil | 36 | Brighouse, England | 7th |
| Baby | 25 | South London, England | 8th |
| Sminty Drop | 23 | Clitheroe, England | 9th |
| Copper Topp | 38 | Cheltenham, England | 10th |
| Starlet | 23 | Surrey, England | 11th |
| Just May | 32 | Essex, England | 12th |

*Information correct at time of filming*

# RUPAUL'S DRAG RACE: UK VS THE WORLD – SEASON ONE

RuPaul's Drag Race: UK vs the World is a spin-off series of RuPaul's Drag Race UK, which premiered on 1st of February 2022. The series features RuPaul as the host and main judge, accompanied by supporting judges Michelle Visage, Graham Norton, and Alan Carr, who return from the original Drag Race UK series. The contestants for the first season were announced on 17th of January 2022.

The production of the series was announced by World of Wonder on 21st of December 2021. The BBC also confirmed that the show would coincide with the relaunch of BBC Three as a television channel. RuPaul's Drag Race: UK vs the World features nine international queens who have previously competed in various editions of the Drag Race franchise worldwide. The filming took place in March 2021 at the same location in Manchester where the third series of RuPaul's Drag Race UK was filmed.

In this series, the two best-performing queens in the "Lip Sync for the World" challenge compete for a gold "RuPeter Badge." The winner of the lip sync not only receives the badge but also has the power to choose which one of the bottom queens to eliminate from the competition.

Blu Hydrangea emerged as the victor in the inaugural season of RuPaul's Drag Race UK vs the World, securing the coveted title. Mo Heart achieved the position of runner-up, displaying impressive talent and skill throughout the competition.

| Contestant | Age | Hometown | Original season(s) | Result |
|---|---|---|---|---|
| Blu Hydrangea | 25 | Belfast, United Kingdom | UK series 1 | Winner |
| Mo Heart | 34 | Kansas City, United States | US season 10 | Runner-up |
| | | | All Stars 4 | |
| Baga Chipz | 31 | London, United Kingdom | UK series 1 | 3rd/4th |
| Jujubee | 36 | Boston, United States | US season 2 | |
| | | | All Stars 1 | |
| | | | All Stars 5 | |
| Janey Jacké | 28 | Volendam, Netherlands | Holland season 1 | 5th |
| Pangina Heals | 32 | Bangkok, Thailand | Drag Race Thailand | 6th |
| Jimbo | 37 | Victoria, Canada | Canada season 1 | 7th |
| Cheryl Hole | 27 | Chelmsford, United Kingdom | UK series 1 | 8th |
| Lemon | 25 | New York City, United States | Canada season 1 | 9th |

## EPISODE ONE: GLOBAL GLAMAZONS

In the exciting premiere of the show, renowned judge RuPaul brings together a group of talented drag queens from around the world for the very first time. Their initial challenge is to create a spectacular royal command performance. With their fate in the competition hanging in the balance, each queen is determined to make a lasting impression as they showcase their unique talents fit for royalty. Adding to the star-studded panel of judges, Spice Girls icon Mel C joins the esteemed panel of Michelle Visage and Graham Norton. As the competition kicks off, the first queen faces elimination, heightening the stakes for all the contestants.

## EPISODE TWO: RUPAUL BALL

As the global Drag Race competition intensifies, the spotlight shines on the RuPaul Ball this week. Paying homage to the legendary RuPaul, the queens are tasked with showcasing their creativity and style through three runway looks. Among these looks is an outfit they must design from scratch, worthy of being worn by the iconic Mama Ru. Adding their expertise to the judging panel, Bafta-winning comedy star Daisy May Cooper joins the esteemed panel of Michelle Visage and Alan Carr. As the competition reaches new heights, another queen must bid farewell and sashay away from the stage.

## EPISODE THREE: WEST END WENDYS

As the competition narrows down to seven global glamazons, the stakes are higher than ever. This week, their stage presence, singing, and dancing abilities are put to the test in a thrilling celebration of musical theatre. The queens take the stage to perform in "West End Wendys - The Rusical." Joining RuPaul, Michelle Visage, and Graham Norton on the judging panel is none other than Jonathan Bailey, the talented star of "Bridgerton" and Olivier Award winner. With the spotlight on their performance, the queens must dazzle the judges and prove they have what it takes to shine in the world of musical theatre.

## EPISODE FOUR: SNATCH GAME

The high-stakes international battle for the title of Queen of the World rages on, and this week brings forth the legendary challenge: the Snatch Game. But there's a twist to this fan-favourite challenge. With iconic team captains Katie Price and Michelle Visage leading the way, the queens step up to the plate to deliver their finest celebrity impressions and display their improvisational skills, all in an effort to bring a smile to Mama Ru's face. The stage is set for laughter, wit, and fierce competition as the queens aim to slay the Snatch Game and secure their spot at the top.

## EPISODE FIVE: SEMIFINALS

In this week's thrilling episode, the queens face an electrifying challenge that puts their singing and dancing skills to the test. They must create their own unique rendition of one of RuPaul's classic hits, pushing their creativity and talent to the limit. Guiding them through the process is the sensational Jade Thirlwall from Little Mix, offering her expert coaching as they hit the recording studio to lay down their vocals. With the stage set, RuPaul, Michelle Visage, and Graham Norton take their seats on the judging panel, ready to witness the queens' performances. As the tension mounts, the fate of yet another queen hangs in the balance, leading to a nail-biting elimination.

## EPISODE SIX: GRAND FINALE

The moment we've all been waiting for has arrived—it's the highly anticipated Grand Finale. After an exhilarating season filled with fierce competition, the workroom welcomed nine iconic queens from around the world, all vying for the coveted title of Queen of the Mothertucking World. Now, after six weeks of challenges, transformations, and unforgettable moments, the time has come for RuPaul to bestow the crown upon one deserving queen. The tension is palpable as we prepare for the ultimate climax of this extraordinary journey. Who will earn the honour of being crowned the winner? The world is about to find out.

# QUIZ

## SEASON ONE

1) **Episode two:** "Downton Draggy" - Scaredy Kat was eliminated, but to which song/band?
2) **Episode four:** "Snatch Game" - who did Divina De Campo and Blu Hydrangea portray?
3) **Episode five:** "Girl Groups Battle Royale" – Team Filth Harmony included which Drag Race contenders?
4) **Episode six:** "Thirsty Werk" - which two queens faced elimination?
5) Who was the guest judge in episode seven: "Family That Drags Together"?

## SEASON TWO

1) **Episode two:** "Rats: The Rusical" - which two queens battled against elimination to the song: "Memory" by Elaine Paige.
2) **Episode four:** "Morning Glory" - the queens served looks in a Monster Mashup runway theme, which three queens were declared 'safe'?
3) **Episode five:** "The RuRuvision Song Contest" - saw the formation of two musical groups, what were their names?
4) **Episode six:** "Snatch Game" – who did Sister Sister and Tayce imitate?
5) **Episode nine:** "BeastEnders" – name the characters played by: Bimini, Ellie Diamond and Lawrence Chaney?

## SEASON THREE

1) How old was Krystal Versace when participating in Season Three?
2) **Episode two:** "Dragoton" – Three teams were created for the main challenge; what were their names?
3) At the time of filming, which location in England was Ella Vaday representing?
4) **Episode six:** "Snatch Game" – Who did River Medway and Choriza May imitate?
5) **Episode eight:** "Bra Wars" (The Fempire Claps Back) name the characters that the following queens portray: Ella Vaday, Kitty Scott-Claus, Krystal Versace and Vanity Milan?

## SEASON FOUR

1) Black Peppa resides in Birmingham, but which country do they originate from?
2) Which queen sent Le Fil home in episode six (and to which song/band)?
3) **Episode one:** "ST4RT Your Engines" – Which queens portrayed: Mr Blobby, Test Card F, Del Boy and Patsy Stone?
4) **Episode three:** "Naff-ta Awards" – Which two queens were paired together to create looks in the colour blue?
5) **Episode nine:** "Comedy Queens" – Who was the guest judge?

# DISCLAIMER

The author is not responsible for any errors or omissions or for any actions taken based on the information contained in this book. This book is provided for informational purposes only, and the author and publisher shall not be liable for any errors or omissions or for any actions taken based on the information contained in this book.

# QUIZ ANSWERS

## SEASON ONE

1) Venus by Bananarama
2) Julia Child and Mary Berry
3) Cheryl Hole, Crystal and The Vivienne
4) Blu Hydrangea and Cheryl Hole
5) Michaela Coel

## SEASON TWO

1) Cherry Valentine and Tayce
2) Ellie Diamond, Tayce and Tia Kofi
3) Bananadrama and United Kingdolls.
4) Sally Morgan and Jane Turner.
5) Scat Slater, Thot Bottom and Phyllis Bitchell.

## SEASON THREE

1) 19
2) Team Ride or Die, Team Ball Busters and Team Babycizers.
3) Dagenham, London
4) Amy Childs and Margarita Pracatan.
5) Daft Shader, Brabarella, She-3PHO and Baby Yolo.

## SEASON FOUR

1) Saint Martin
2) Black Peppa (Stop by The Spice Girls)
3) Black Peppa, Cheddar Gorgeous, Pixie Polite and Patsy Stone.

**4)** Le Fil and Sminty Drop.
**5)** Olly Alexander

Printed in Dunstable, United Kingdom